THE QUIET CENTER

JOHN C. LILLY, M.D.

PHILIP HANSEN BAILEY LILLY

RONIN PUBLISHING
BERKELEY, CA

THE QUIET CENTER

ISBN: 1-57951-059-0

Copyright © 2003 by Philip Hansen Bailey

Published by

RONIN Publishing, Inc.

PO Box 22900

Oakland, CA 94609

www.roninpub.com

Credits:

Editors:	**Beverly A. Potter** www.docpotter.com
	Lance Tilford
Copy Editor:	**Amy Demmon**
Cover:	**Judy July,** Generic Typograpy

Fonts - text:	Avant Garde
	Copperplate Gothic
	Hypnotica
	Palatino
	Skia

Distributed to the trade by **Publishers Group West**

Printed in the United States of America by McNaughton & Gunn

Library of Congress Card Number —2003092593

Printing Number 1

Acknowledgments

To our friends:

Ann and Jerry Moss

Rudi Vogt

Dr. Albert Hofmann

John Allen

The October Gallery

Faustin Bray

Brian Wallace

Creon Levitt

Barry King

Timothy Leary

Oscar and Kathy Janiger

Roberta Goodman

Thomas Welch

Jim Suhre and Kate

Bob and Denny

Adam Trombly

Larry and Char Raithaus

Gessie Houghton, Divyam Preaux,
        and Jean Francois

Glenn and Lee Perry at Samadhi Tank

And family:

Mary and Charles Lilly

Lisa Lyon Lilly and Barbara Clarke Lilly

Evelyn and George Musser

William, Kevin, Cherie and David Bailey

The highest topic
of research
is our consciousness.
John Lilly is a pioneer
in modern consciousness
research.

—Albert Hoffman

TABLE OF CONTENTS

Books by John Lilly

Communications Between Man & Dolphin
The Possibilities of Talking with Other Species

Deep Self
Profound Relaxation
and the Tank Isolation Technique

Lilly on Dolphins
Humans of the Sea

Man and Dolphins

Simulations of God
The Science of Belief

The Center of the Cyclone
An Autobiography of Inner Space

The Dyadic Cyclone
The Autobiography of a Couple

The Dolphin in History

The Mind of the Dolphin
On Nonhuman Intelligence

The Scientist
A Metaphysical Autobiography

Programming and Metaprogramming
the Human Biocomputer

The Quiet Center

Survival Guide

Y OU ARE HOLDING A SURVIVAL GUIDE for the body, mind, and spirit. The quiet center is that quiet place within us that must be experienced to realize a more fully conscious life. Turning off the outside stimulus of sound, light, and activity, the human mind rests in a profound state of relaxation, contributing toward the possibility of significant visionary experience. Practitioners of these states of being provide awe-inspiring tales of profound relaxation and grand out-of-body visionary experiences. So whether it is stress relief that is being sought after or contact with higher levels of consciousness, there is something here for everyone.

Garnered from decades of research and experiments, this material is provided as a doorway to unlock realities that have yet to be seen and as a tool to get to where you are going from here.

—Philip Hansen Bailey Lilly

Hawaii

THOUGHTS ON LILLY

S OMETIME IN THE SIXTIES, the term "far out" acquired a positive connotation. It still meant something or someone removed from the mainstream, but in those exploratory, innovative times that had come to be an accolade rather than an insult. In the context, then, I regarded Dr. John Lilly as the most "far out" person on the planet. Seeming to operate with absolute fearlessness, he allowed his massive intellect and consummate erudition to carry him to one frontier, one edge after another, regardless of the psychological and even physical risks involved. And like the god Hermes, who must have been his personal deity, he brought things back from out beyond the boundaries, gave them back to us, and wryly observed the way they changed our lives. If the changes were controversial, so much the better. Every bit as much as he loved the truth, and was willing to go to any lengths to pursue it, he also loved the thrill of dropping those truths like cherry bombs into the tepid punchbowl of polite science. I'd like to think that somewhere, in another dimension perhaps, this great man is astride a dolphin, leaping over paradigm and convention, riding headlong and joyful into some ultimate Ultimate where he, more than any man I've ever known, will feel completely at home.

—Tom Robbins

FROM SCIENCE TO GOD

W HAT IS CONSCIOUSNESS? And where does it come from? As far as Western science is concerned, consciousness is a great enigma. That we are conscious beings is the most obvious fact of our existence. Yet there is nothing more difficult to explain. Why should the complex processing of information in the brain result in a corresponding experience? There is nothing in physics, chemistry, biology, or any other science that predicts any of us should have an interior world. Paradoxically, science would be much happier if there were no such thing as consciousness—yet without consciousness there would be no science.

Today, largely as a result of a growing understanding of the human brain, a number of psychologists and philosophers are investigating the mystery of consciousness. Some believe that a deeper understanding of brain chemistry will explain how consciousness arises. Others look to quantum physics. Some explore cybernetics; others find sources of hope in chaos theory. Yet whatever idea is put forward, one thorny question remains unanswered: How can something as immaterial as consciousness ever arise from something as unconscious as matter?

> We are like the medieval astronomers who tried in vain to explain the irregular motion of the planets.

In my book *From Science to God*, I propose that we are in a situation similar to that of the medieval astronomers who tried in vain to explain the irregular motion of the planets with a complex system of circles rolling around circles. Copernicus realized that if the Earth were not the center of the universe but a planet orbiting the sun, then the wandering motion of the planets could be easily explained. But the Church did not take kindly to his ideas. Giordano Bruno was burned at the stake in Rome for supporting the Copernican model (and for referring to God as "she"), while Galileo was put under house arrest for the remainder of his life.

In present times we may be approaching a similar paradigm shift with regard to consciousness. Most scientists assume that consciousness emerges in some way or other from brain activity. But if this approach is getting us nowhere, perhaps we should consider an alternative worldview—one found in many metaphysical and spiritual traditions, where consciousness is held to be an essential quality of the cosmos, as fundamental as space, time, and matter.

> If we want to find God, we need to look into the realm of "deep mind"—a realm that science has only begun to explore.

Interestingly, expanding our worldview to include consciousness as a fundamental quality does not actually threaten any of the conclusions of modern science. Mathematics remains the same, as do physics, biology, chemistry, and all our other discoveries about the material world. What changes is our understanding of ourselves. If consciousness is indeed fundamental, then the teachings of the great sages and mystics begin to make new sense.

Those who have penetrated to the core of their minds have frequently discovered a profound connection with the ground of all being. The sense of being an individual self—that feeling of I-ness that we all know so well but find so hard to define—turns out to be not so unique after all. They claim repeatedly that the light of consciousness shining in me as my self is the same light that shines in you and in every other sentient being.

Some have expressed this realization in the statement "I am God." To modern science, such statements are nothing more than self-delusion. Physicists have looked out into deep space to the edges of the universe, back into "deep time" to the beginning of creation, and down into "deep structure" to the fundamental constituents of matter. The majority have found not only no evidence for God, but no need for God. The Universe seems to work perfectly well without any divine assistance.

But when mystics speak of the divine, they are not speaking of some supernatural being who rules the workings of the universe; they are talking of the world within. If we want to find God, we need to look into the realm of "deep mind"—a realm that science has only begun to explore. As we learn more, we may find that we have embarked on a course that will lead not only to a much fuller understanding of ourselves, but also to that long-sought synthesis of science and spirit.

—Peter Russell
Author of
From Science to God
The Mystery of Consciousness
www.peterussell.com

Reprinted by permission from NAPRA Review
July/Aug 2002 www.napra.com

We shall meet somewhere in Alternity. . . .

**John Lilly—scientist, mystic,
and consciousness explorer.
1915 to 2001**

1
SEARCH FOR SELF

EACH ONE OF US IS FAR GREATER, far more advanced, far more consciously aware, far more intelligent than we conceive of our Selves as being. Within each of us is a central low pressure place—a Quiet Center—in which we can learn to live eternally. Just outside of this quiet center is a cyclone, the rotating storm of your ego, competing with other egos in a furious high-velocity circular dance.

In the quiet center we are untouched by the cyclone, but as we leave it, the roar of the rotating wind deafens as we join the frenzied dance of our ever more busy lives. Our centered thinking-feeling-being, our Satori, is in the quiet center, not outside in the busy world. Our pushed-pulled-driven states, our anti-Satori modes of functioning, our self-created hell, is outside the quiet center. When in the quiet center we are off the wheel of karma, outside the busy details and dramas of life, rising to join the Creators of the Universe—the Creators of us. Here we find that we have created Them who are Us

Major philosophical puzzles are concerned with the existence of Self, with the relation of the Self to the brain, to the mind, to other minds—with the existence or non-existence of an immortal Self. Powerful beliefs have evolved about these areas of thought.

Two Selves

THERE ARE TWO ASPECTS OF THE SELF. There is an observing
Self—the Observer—and a doing or participating Self—
the Operator. The whole Self is the Observer-Operator.
Depending upon circumstances, the Observer can be
observing external events, or internal events, or both.
The Operator can be participating in external events, or
in internal events, or both. In the external reality the
Operator uses the body to do things and participate. In
the internal reality the Operator uses "simulations" of
reality, which are concepts, beliefs, meta-beliefs, inten-
tions, distinctions, and so forth. These internal images or
pictures of external reality are not "real," they are facsimiles—simulations—of what is out there, as we perceive it. Simulations of the same
external event can vary widely among
people.

The Observer
is always
watching.

No matter what you are doing the
Observer-Operator—the Self—is
always immersed in the internal
simulations domain. Even when engaged in external
events, you are simultaneously engaged in watching and
acting in the internal domain. The two "realities," internal and external, interact in a two-way feedback relationship—internal reality to external reality to internal reality
to external reality and so on endlessly.

Larger Forces

LIKE A SCIENTIST, THE SELF OBSERVES, which involves consciousness and control. In the science game, the scientist
is expected to be always conscious, aware and in control
of his thinking—to be rational—and in control of the
processes that he is examining. This is not always the
case. When in the void space and isolated from sensory
stimulation, such as when in a floatation tank, I discovered that there are many states in which the Self is not in
control but is being programmed by forces very much
larger than Self.

It is as if the Self is a victim, being coercively persuaded of another belief system not one's own. Most of us have been aware of such an experience at one time or another, especially as children. The passive Observer and the active Operator both disappear under these conditions. Interlocked with forces, with beings, with entities far greater than we are, the Self does that which it is programmed to do rather than to operate by our own initiative. We are forced into participation by external forces. We do not sit still and watch, as a scientist would.

The Search for Reality

CAN THE MIND RENDER ITSELF SUFFICIENTLY OBJECTIVE to study itself? Can we use the mind to ponder on the mind? It is perfectly feasible for the intellect to grasp the fact that the physiological changes of the brain occur simultaneously with thought. On the other hand, the mind has difficulty conceiving of the connection between its own thoughts and these changes. The difficulties of the precise relation between the two have caused many controversies as to which is the more "real"— objective or subjective reality.

> Can we use the mind to ponder on the mind?

Words, language, logic, and mathematical descriptions are not adequate expressers of either the inner or outer aspects of reality. Somehow, all descriptions of reality are sterile. They tend to play word games, that cleverly juggle with ideas in intricate patterns as if meaningful.

I've searched for the answer to the question "What is reality?" I sought an answer in the study of mathematics, of logic, of semantics, for example. Each proved to be sterile in the deeper search, yet helpful in widening my representational capacities to see relations internally into my own mind. Skill in manipulating concepts, no matter how precise, no matter how inclusive, can not answer this pressing question.

Few Tools

THERE ARE PROTOCOLS FOR HOW TO THINK OBJECTIVELY about outer physical-chemical-biological realities. Equally important is to develop ways to think objectively about the inner realities. But we lack tools to conduct a truly objective philosophical analysis of who we are on the inside. I devoted much of my scientific career to this challenge.

> We lack tools to conduct a truly objective philosophical analysis of who we are on the inside.

I sought answers in experimental and theoretical physics. In cosmogony, the study of the origins of the cosmos, where the universe raised her lovely head. For a time I was entranced—in trance—with the seductions of astrophysics, astronomy, and so forth. The study of submicroscopic realms of matter—quantum mechanics—seduced me, as did the study of known physical energy—light, photons, and thermodynamics.

Finally I came to the study of my own brain and its contained-restrained mind and I took a new direction into new domains. I returned to ponder my earlier insight that the physiological changes of the brain occur simultaneously with thought, but it cannot conceive of the connection between its own thoughts and these changes. I wondered how can one make these connections? How can one make an objective record of these changes in the brain and the corresponding thoughts?

Better Method

AS A DEDICATED YOUNG EXPERIMENTAL SCIENTIST I saw a possible means of recording "the physiological changes of the brain." The cutting edge research at that time was that of Lord Edgar Adrian who had written a paper, "The Spread of Electrical Activity in the Cerebral Cortex." I determined to devise a better method of recording the electrical activity that yielded a more complete picture of the electrical activity throughout the brain, not just in small areas of the cortex.

My objective was to learn more of the mind in the brain—its thoughts, their changes, their "sources and sinks"—in order to devise a method of recording its activities simultaneously with the changes in the brain. I was seeking an objective method to fast record the activities of the brain while simultaneously making objective fast recording of the activities of the mind in that brain.

I continued the search, in neuroanatomy, neurology, neurosurgery, psychiatry where I found more data but no new methods. The methods used in these disciplines where as limited as those I'd explored in other fields. Spoken and written language, mostly in the form of questions, were used to probe the mind, while EEGs and fast electrical recordings were the tools used to explore the brain. There was no method of recording the mind activities and the brain activities simultaneously. Most medical researchers did not feel that there was any hope of ever accomplishing this difficult task.

I devised new methods of recording the electrical activity of the brain in many places simultaneously, recorded and reproduced on a two-dimensional array. I worked out new, safer ways of placing small electrodes within the brain. But I abandoned this avenue of research when I realized that there was no way of recording the activities of the brain without altering, and often injuring, the structure of the brain itself, and thereby changing the capacities of the mind.

Fascinations

OF PARTICULAR INTEREST TO ME are the domains represented by the mathematical concepts of zero—the origin at which numbers and variables cease having any value; of infinity—the non-terminus approaching in which, numbers and variables assume values that cannot yet be represented; of the point—the smallest possible value of any number or of any variable that approaches, but does not reach, zero; of various differential operators such as V2 = 0, for example, which can move through their defined domains free of constraints by the domain in and upon which they operate.

I am fascinated with the relation of identity, how one variable relates to another, in the consciously functioning domain. Assuming your conscious Self to have a "size" in a certain domain—say equivalent to that of a human brain in the external **Identify** reality domain, you probably identify **your whole** your Self with that size. Start cutting **Self with a** down that size until you are a point. In **point.** any domain, a point is not zero. Identify your whole Self with a point. This kind of point has consciousness, memory, and the complete knowledge of the individual Self. It can remain a fixed point in a defined domain, a moving point in the same domain, or a point in any domain. Such a point has no mass, no charge, no spin, no gravitational constant and, hence, is free to move in any physical field.

And so on and on for identities of Self with differential Operators, with infinities, with zero. Identify Self with a differential Operator that can move through a field unconstrained by the presence of the field. Assume that you are infinite. What is the experience? Assume you are zero. What is the experience? I leave you with these exercises to perform on—and in—yourself.

Meta-Transformation

SOME RESEARCHERS END THEIR BOOKS—and apparently their search—with pessimistic statements. For example Ludwig Wittgenstein, a foremost thinker, said in *Tractatus Logico-Philosophicus*: "There are, indeed, things that cannot be put into words. They make

themselves manifest. They are what is mystical."
Wittgenstein's statement can be transformed into the
explorer's domain by inserting a few critical words.
"There are, indeed, things that *as yet* cannot be put into
words *by other means*. They make themselves manifest." In place of "They are what is mystical" we can
substitute, "They are now what is in the Unknown yet
to be found."

This is how I operate. If I see premature closing off
of possibilities, as if something is impossible—mystical—I paraphrase and reorient the statements to
continue my own metabelief that the province of the
mind has no limits. Its own contained beliefs set limits
that can be transcended by suitable metabeliefs like the
one in this example.

Returning to the *Tractatus*, there is an oft-quoted
statement, "Whereof one cannot speak, thereof one
must be silent." By adding the words "as yet"—
"Whereof one cannot speak *as yet*, thereof one must be
silent"—the statement is transformed into an opening
injunction, rather than, as it is given by Wittgenstein,
an absolute closure of a system of thought by this
injunction. Of that which we cannot yet speak, we
remain silent until a new experience or way of expression allows us to speak. Radio waves in 1700 A.D.
were silent, for example.

G. Spencer Brown, who investigated the basis of
reality, shows in *Laws of Form* that Wittgenstein probably was referring to descriptive language rather than
injunctive or instructional language. Injunctive language instructs on how to do, or to make, or to create
something in the inner reality and/or in the external
reality. Wittgenstein did not have modern neurophysi-
ological knowledge nor computers, each of which
directly opens the descriptive and injunctive domains
expressible in new languages. Experimental science
somehow seems to topple previously expressed abso-
lutes about reality, about meaning, about language,

about perception, about cognition, about creating
descriptions of minds with limits, specified by the
constructor-descriptor. However, the limits defined are
only in the description used, in the simulations or
models of the mind doing the describing.

Lack of Limits

REALIZATION OF THE LACK OF ANY LIMITS IN THE MIND is not
easy to acquire. The domains of direct experience of
infinities within greater infinities of experience are
sometimes frightening, sometimes "awe-full," sometimes "bliss-full." I quote from Franklin Merrell-Wolff,
*The Philosophy of Consciousness Without an Object:
Reflections on the Nature of Transcendental Consciousness,*
who feels this lack of mind limits in his own experiences.

*1. The first discernible effect in consciousness
was something that I may call a shift in the base
of consciousness. From the relative point of
view, the final step may be likened to a leap into
Nothing. At once, that Nothing was resolved
into utter Fullness, which in turn gave the
relative world a dreamlike quality of unreality. I
felt and knew myself to have arrived, at last, at
the Real. I was not dissipated in a sort of spatial
emptiness, but on the contrary was spread out
in a Fullness beyond measure.*

*The roots of my consciousness, which prior to
this moment had been (seemingly) more or less
deeply implanted in the field of relative consciousness, now were forcibly removed and
instantaneously transplanted into a supernal
region. This sense of being thus transplanted
has continued to the present day, and it seems
to be a much more normal state of emplacement
than ever the old rooting had been.*

2. *Closely related to the foregoing is a transformation in the meaning of the "Self," or "I."*
Previously, pure subjectivity had seemed to me to be like a zero or vanishing point, a "somewhat" that had position in consciousness but no body. So long as that which man calls his "Self" had body, it stood within the range of analytic observation. Stripping off the sheaths of this body until none is left is the function of the discriminative technique in meditation. At the end there remains that which is never an object and yet is the foundation upon which all relative consciousness is strung like beads upon a string.

As a symbol to represent this ultimate and irreducible subject to all consciousness, the "I" element, I know nothing better than zero or an evanescent point. The critical stage in the transformation is the realization of the "I" as zero. But, at once, that "I" spreads out into an unlimited "thickness." It is as though the "I" became the whole of space. The Self is no longer a pole or focal point, but it sweeps outward, everywhere, in a sort of unpolarized consciousness, which is at once Self-identity and the objective content of consciousness. It is an unequivocal transcendence of the subject-object relationship. Herein lies the rationale of the inevitable ineffability of mystical insight. All language is grounded in the subject-object relationship, and so, at best, can only misrepresent transcendent consciousness when an effort is made to express its immediately given value.

His last statement can be transformed by means present in his own writings into, once again, a transforming injunction. *That* language—not *all* language—grounded in the subject-object relationship misrepresents transcendent consciousness when, in that language, an effort is made to express the immediately given value of transcendent consciousness.

G. Spencer Brown's doorway out of this dilemma is the development of an injunctive language that gives instructions suitable to the listener—the reader or experiencer—on how to evoke-enter-create transcendent consciousness in your Self. I have found Merrell-Wolff's writings on his own experience to have injunctive qualities for me, for changing my "subject-object" consciousness into the new domains that he so beautifully expresses.

Exploration Discouraged

I WOULD LIKE TO END THIS DISCUSSION WITH A QUOTATION from *Laws of Form*:

> *Unfortunately we find systems of education today that have departed so far from the plain truth, that they now teach us to be proud of what we know and ashamed of ignorance. This is doubly corrupt. It is corrupt not only because pride is in itself a mortal sin, but also because to teach pride in knowledge is to put up an effective barrier against any advance upon what is already known, since it makes one ashamed to look beyond the bonds imposed by one's ignorance.*

To any person prepared to enter with respect into the realm of his great and universal ignorance, the secrets of being will eventually unfold, and they will do so in a measure according to his freedom from natural and indoctrinated shame in his respect of their revelation.

To arrive at the simplest truth, as Newton knew and practiced, requires years of contemplation. Not activity. Not reasoning. Not calculating. Not busy behaviour of any kind. Not reading. Not talking. Not making an effort. Not thinking. Simply bearing in mind what it is one needs to know. And yet those with the courage to tread this path to real discovery are not only offered practically no guidance on how to do so, they are actively discouraged and have to set about it in secret, pretending meanwhile to be diligently engaged in the frantic diversions and to conform with the deadening personal opinions which are being continually thrust upon them.

In these circumstances, the discoveries that any person is able to undertake represent the places where, in the face of induced psychosis, he has, by his own faltering and unaided efforts, returned to sanity. Painfully, and even dangerously, maybe. But nonetheless returned, however furtively.

2

WHAT IS REALITY?

TURNED MY ATTENTION TO THE STUDY and development
of the mind—*my mind*. I studied semantics, logic,
mathematics, means of modeling the brain's and the
mind's activities. Warren McCulloch and Heinz Von
Foerster were working in the area of representation of
the brain's activities and I studied their work. For the
mind studies, I needed more "new data." I pursued
psychoanalysis in depth. I found a psychoanalyst's
psychoanalyst Robert Waelder, who had a Ph.D. in
Physics and trained with Anna and Sigmund Freud in
Vienna, Austria. I worked with Dr. Waelder for three
years, five to seven days a week, one hour a day. I
found much that was pertinent to my pursuit of the
question, "What is reality?"

I confirmed that wholly complex domains of
thought, feeling, doing, and memory operating below
my levels of awareness programmed my beliefs about
"what is real." Inner reality has its own laws, distinct
from, and many times counter to, the laws of outer
reality. I struggled with the theories—belief systems—
of others in regard to the nature of inner reality. With
Waelder's help and quiet acceptance, I was able to
enter new inner domains of feeling, thinking and
emoting to be able to represent the experiences verbally in writing.

As my modeling of inner reality became more
open, my respect for the Unknown in my own mind
increased greatly. I discovered that the depths of mind

are as great as the depths of cosmic outer space. There
are inner universes as well as outer ones. My concept
of meta-beliefs—beliefs about beliefs—as the limiting
beliefs that restrain, confining and limit the processes
operations of my mind originated during my work
with Robert Waelder.

Sensory Isolation

PARALLEL WITH THE BRAIN-ACTIVITY STUDIES, I conducted
mind research in the sensory void environment of the
"flotation tank," sometimes also called the "isolation
tank." Why is sensory isolation necessary for the study
of mind? My reasoning was founded on a basic tenet
of physics, biology, and other experimental sciences. In
order to adequately study a system, all known influences to and from that system must either be attenuated below threshold for excitation, reliably accounted
for, or eliminated to avoid unplanned disturbances of
that system. Disturbances from unknown sources may
then be found and dealt with more adequately.

Using this injunction from experimental science, I
decided to isolate my body-brain-mind from external
reality, insofar as this was possible
without damaging it with chemicals. I decided to
To study my own mind, it must be isolate my
isolated from all known "sources" of body-brain-
stimulation and from "sinks" of mind from
reaction in the here-and-now exter- external
nal reality. To achieve this I devised reality.
the void method using the sensory
isolation tank for the study of my own mind. It is a
method for an isolated mind to study its own processes, free of feedback with the external world. Quite
quickly I found this method gave a new source of data
of great richness.

Once you have been deep in your deeper and
deeper Self—it deepens at every exposure to the
sensory void—your ability to transmit the data must

also be increased. I found that most other minds are not prepared to hear—to understand and grasp—what it means to explore and be immersed in such depths of the Self. Certain domains of the mind, certain states of being, certain states of one's own consciousness, are so foreign-alien-weird-strange-unfamiliar to most other minds that they cannot listen to or read what I say or write without becoming upset, or without using ready labels for the explorer, rendering my efforts to communicate either negative or null.

Isolating Brain and Mind

AT THE TIME THAT I BEGAN MY RESEARCH there were two schools of thought about the origins of conscious activity within the brain. The first school hypothesized that the brain needed stimilation from external reality to keep its conscious states going. This school maintained that sleep resulted as soon as the brain was freed of external stimulation. When one retired to bed in darkness of the night and the silence of the bedroom, the rational mind automatically went to sleep as a result of its release from the necessity of carrying on transactions with the external world.

The second school maintained that the activities of brain were inherently autorhythmic. In other words, within brain substance itself were cells that tended to continue their ossicillations without the necessity of any external stimuli. According to this interpretation, the origins of consciousness were in natural rhythms of the brain's cell circuitry.

I contemplated the literature, talked to people involved in these two schools of thought, and decided to test the rival hypotheses. I reviewed what was known about sleep, anesthesia, coma, accidental injury to the brain, and other causes for the apparent cessation of consciousness in human beings.

I looked at the physics and the biophysics of stimulation of the body and considered what, according to scientific consensus, was thought to stimulate a body. I considered the effects of light and its stimulation of the eyes. I considered sound and its stimulation of the ears, touch, and pressure and their stimulation of the skin and deep-lying end organs within the body. I took a good look at the effects of gravitation and its determination of body position and motion. I looked at temperature differences, at clothing, at the effects of heat and cold.

Key Experiment

I REALIZED THAT THE KEY EXPERIMENT must cut down the various forms of stimulation of the body to the minimum possible value, short of cutting nerve fibers going to the brain. I realized the essential feedback relationship between motion of the body and its self-stimulation during motion—the feedback from muscles, joints, bones, and skin.

I then devised a set of standards for isolating the body from all known forms of physical stimulation. I reasoned that sound and light could be eliminated by well-known methods using unlit soundproof chambers. Motion of the body could be eliminated by voluntary effort with relaxation in the horizontal, gravitational, equipotential plane. The usual bedroom situation, lying horizontal on a bed in a dark, silent room, satisfied these criteria of isolation.

The key experiment required cutting out all stimulation.

The remaining sources of stimulation, however, were more difficult to remove. When you are lying on a bed, the antigravity pressures on the surface of your body against the bed generate a stagnation of the blood flow to the skin and muscles on the underside of the body. This leads to stimulation which causes the body to turn during the night to relieve the slow flowing of the blood in those tissues under pressure on the bed.

The second group of stimuli which were not satisfied by the bed in the dark, silent room were those of temperature differences—a flow of air as a result of the convection currents over the body cools those parts exposed to the air. Those parts not exposed to air remain warm; in fact, they may become too warm as a result of the local metabolism of the tissues not exposed to the air. The tactile stimulation of the body against the bed and of the coverings over the body would also have to be eliminated.

Water Flotation

AFTER A LONG AND PROTRACTED STUDY of these various sources stimulation, I received an inspiration to attempt the use of water flotation. Water would have the advantage of supporting the body without stimulating the skin if there were motion of the body itself, or if the water relative to the body, the water temperature were adjusted to soak up the heat given off by the metabolism of the body and the brain, the temperature problem could be solved. Changes in temperature along body axis and over the surface of the skin could be reduced below the level at which they stimulated the end organs of the skin. The gravitational counterforces supporting the body would also be reduced by flotation below the level at which they could be detected by the end organs and the central nervous system of the body itself.

I visualized a tank in which the body could be supported in water that would be maintained at the proper temperature to take care of the generation of heat within the body. This tank would be in a soundproof chamber which could be blacked out. I sketched out the necessary apparatus and began to talk to my colleagues in the National Institutes of Health about this proposal.

I realized that in order to furnish air to the person submerged in the water, I would need to draw upon the knowledge of respiratory apparatus learned during World War II in my high-altitude research. The person immersed would need a breathing mask which must be as nonstimulating as possible to the head and face. The apparatus would have to furnish air—the oxygen in the air—and get rid of the carbon dioxide given off by the lungs as a result of the metabolism of the body burning the oxygen.

I talked the proposal over with my immediate superior, who suggested that I go to the National Institute of Arthritis and Metabolic Diseases where a man had worked with respiratory systems during World War II for the Office of Naval Research. The flotation tank was born.

Research Disavowed

MANY OF MY COLLEAGUES DISAVOWED ME and my research. I understand their belief systems and the power such systems have over our minds. I do not recriminate them, nor do I blame former friends for not maintaining contact with me. In my search for reality, I have driven myself and hence close associates, relatives and friends to the brink of the loss of all communicational contacts for months at a time, by means totally alien to the previously accepted belief systems in our culture. I voluntarily entered into domains forbidden by a large fraction of those in our culture who are not curious, are not explorative, and are not mentally equipped to enter these domains.

When Gary Schwartz, a University of Arizona scientist, was asked about his controlled studies of mediums, whose side he was on—the mediums or the skeptics, he answered,

*"Well, I'm not on either side. I'm on the side of
the data. If the data takes me to the mediums, I
go to the mediums. If the data takes me to the
skeptics, I go to the skeptics. Now, if you ask
me whose world view I prefer, there's no question that the medium's is much more beautiful
and special. But my job is not to test my beliefs.
It's to follow the data. Are we trying to prove
the survival of consciousness? No. What we're
trying to do is allow survival of consciousness
to prove itself. If mediums are willing to stand
up and be counted, scientists should be willing
to stand up and count them."*

—John Edward
Crossing Over

Difficult Search

MY OWN MIND PROVIDED ITS OWN DIFFICULTIES in this search.
There were times when I felt the search must stop. It is
too much to ask of my biology as a human; it was too
much to ask of my functioning as a social being in the
world of humankind with its neglected suffering
millions of humans. I took time for the search away
from other activities. In my search for the bases of
reality I minimized participation in the social reality,
limited it, insofar as this was possible, to communication of the results of the search. Eventually, I saw that
this dilemma was a distraction, a seduction enticing
me away from the search.

My life was lived continuously in the search. At
times my efforts were hidden. I could not expose the
experiments to the gaze of others without irreversibly
altering the experimental conditions and thus changing the results with the changed conditions.

In the search there were many times of great joy, of breakthroughs into new domains, of a new grasp of the previously ungraspable. Internally, in the privacy of my own mind, I felt infinitely rewarded by the results.

Many others have pursued the search for reality and its representations. I owe many debts to those who cleared some of the jungles of beliefs, who removed accumulated layers of nonsense before I started digging. I feel somewhat like the sparrows I watched in Minnesota as a boy. Unerringly each sparrow found the undigested edible single kernels of grain in the drying manure. If only it were so easy for us to find the viable kernels of true knowledge in the masses of nonsense given us in books, in the media, in political speeches, in ourselves by ourselves!

3
HUMAN BIO-COMPUTERS

A LL HUMAN BEINGS, all persons who reach adult-hood in the world today are programmed bio-computers. No one of us can escape our own nature as programmable entities. Each of us may literally be our programs—nothing more, nothing less.

The human brain is a living computer with un-known properties—abiocomputer. Its properties are only dimly understood. Its programs for fear, for anger, for love, for pleasure, for pain built are into its structure, its circuitry. Circuits for all these feelings are primitive, inherited in the genetic code.

The mind is the software of that biocomputer. The Observer located in that brain is the result of the brain's computations. As pain and pleasure are inalter-ably linked in the biofeedback of the brain with the body, so is the Observer computed in the large cerebral cortex.

The Observer is a programmer resident in the brain. The programmer is the agent within the brain. The self is the operator contained within the brain in self-reflexive circuitry in the cerebral cortex.

Is the Self immersed in the brain anything more than the computed result of the brain's software? Is the mind anything more than the computational activities of the brain?

Hardwired Programs

DESPITE THE INFINITE VARIETIES OF PROGRAMS AVAILABLE, most of us have a limited set of programs. Some of these are built-in—hardwired. In the simpler basic forms, the programs were mostly built-in. From genetic codes fully-formed organisms are created. The structure of our nervous system reflects its origins in simpler forms of organisms from sessile protozoans, sponges, and corals through sea worms, reptiles, and proto-mammals to primates to apes to early anthropoids to humanoids to human. The patterns of action-reaction are determined by necessities of survival, of adaptation to slow environmental changes, and of passing on the code to descendents.

As the size and complexity of the nervous system and its bodily carrier increase, new levels of programmability appeared, not tied to immediate survival and reproduction. The hardwired programs survived as a basic underlying context for the new levels. Eventually, the cerebral cortex appeared as an expanding high-level operating system controlling the structurally lower levels of the nervous system—the hardwired programs. This made learning and faster adaptation to a changing environment possible. As the new cortex expanded over several millions of years, a critical size of cortex was reached and languages and its consequences appeared.

Repetition

ONE PROBLEM IN HUMAN EXISTENCE is the tendency to repeat. We repeat feeling, thinking, action again and again and again, in the same kind of looping cycle. It is as if we are controlled by a set of loops of tape. On these tapes are recorded what you say on one track and what you feel on another track and what you do on a third track. These are endless loops and you tend to repeat these again and again and again.

By using repeating words, repeating sentences, and repeating ideas, you can get involved in such repetition processes. Traps, blind alleys, evasions, hindrances, and refusals can develop in

We are controlled by our repetitions. response to externally forced repetition. You can become more aware of the repetition processes occurring in you body, in your mind, and in your

feelings, and in your relationships with others. Can you see how you avoid achieving your goals by repetitive methods? How your relationships with others repeat? How you use them in the service of blindly repeating patterns?

Our impulses tend to push us around in such circles, especially if there are two forces operating, two impulses, one counter to the other, in a so-called double bind, you can go circular indefinitely under two counter acting opposing forces. Our need for repetition is such that we tend to repeat in order to be safe. What is familiar is safe. The safety of the old tape loops rotate merrily. Under these circumstances, we tend to ignore the possibilities of widening out our responses.

Learning to Learn

THE HIGHER-ORDER LEVEL OF STRUCTURE enabled a new capability to emerge—learning to learn. When learning to learn, we make models, use symbols, analogize, create metaphors. In short, we invent and use language, mathematics, art, politics, business, and so forth. This process is called *meta-programming*. Meta-programming appears at a critical cortical size—the cerebral computer must have a large enough number of interconnected circuits of sufficient quality for the operations of meta-programming to exist in the bio-computer.

Reframing

AN ESSENTIAL SET IN LEARNING-TO-LEARN is setting aside
previous limits upon domain exploration and dropping outmoded beliefs about inner and outer realities.
You must examine beliefs about beliefs—*metabeliefs*—
especially those about the limits of your mind. You
must drop the usual self-limiting languages found in
the external reality and escape entrancement—seduction by systems of thought, by other persons, by
successes and failures in the consensus realities of
others linked to your Self as well as of your Self in
those realities. This is the process of embracing a new
paradigm, of thinking outside of the box, of
reframing.

Interlock

INTERLOCK IS THAT SET OF PHENOMENA experienced when
people engage in a two-way communication link.
Examples of external reality interlocks are a conversation between two persons alone with one another, a
telephone conversation, here-and-now sexual relations, a group playing a game or singing together or
working together. In the void state a person's internal
reality can be made up of external reality interlock
simulations, such as when thinking about things
outside of the void space or what happened in the
past.

   Interlock varies in its intensity. In here-and-now
sexual relations, the two bodies—along with their
respective internal realities—interlock at a very high
energy level. In a telephone conversation the interlock
with the other person is weaker in its intensity. In a
court of law, the interlocks between the various ago-
nists are usually of high intensity.

   Any external reality interlock involves two-way
exchanges that originate in the two Observer-Opera-

tors—the two Selves—through facsimiles of shared external and internal reality simulations in the internal realities of each person. Such simulations include language they each use, the simulation of each by the other, the self-simulations of each of their respective roles in the interlock, the simulations of consensus reality they each hold, and the positive, negative, and neutral energy controls exerted by each person involved in the exchange.

For interlock between two persons, the language requirements are limiting in certain domains. In part interlock is comprised of the verbal-vocal language, including control of voice and size of vocabulary, and the levels of cognition expressible by each person. Direct body language, such as facial expressiveness, control of movements of the arms, hands, and body, is deeply involved in face-to-face interlock. Physical contact introduces additional parameters within each person's internal experience of the interlock.

Our simulation of others control what we say. If we expect negative energy from another person in a certain domain of discourse, we tend to avoid that domain, or we may challenge a person to enter into it. If we expect high positive energy from another person, we may avoid that domain or challenge the person. With certain people we expect neutral energy in most domains. For example, if your simulation of another person places him or her above or below your Self in regard to knowledge, ignorance, power, money, sex, or intelligence, you will operate with certain scripts assigned by consensus reality for such interlocks. If your metabelief operator says that interlocks with another person can transcend expected limits, you can move beyond that which you expect of the person. Your simulation of another person can be a catalyst for opening up him or her and oneself into new domains of interlock.

Interlock with Non-Humans

THE INTERLOCK CONCEPT CAN BE EXTENDED beyond
human-human feedback such as to human-dolphin
interlock or to human-canine interlock for example.
Human-machine interlock is everywhere in our culture. For example, the driver-automobile interlock is a
daily occurrence in our lives. The programmer-
computer interlock has assumed
tremendous importance and influences paper-film-tape realities in
powerful ways. Mass production
depends upon exact human-machine
interlocks of diverse types.

> We depend
> on our
> interlocks with
> machines to
> survive.

Our culture is dependent upon
such interlocks. From a person working with a sewing
machine, an author with a laptop, a steel worker in a
mill, a person on an electronic assembly line, a pilot in
a transport jet, a scientist with an electron microscope,
a newscaster with the TV camera and cameramen, to a
user of the computer network, our culture is a large
system of human-machine interlocks generating much
of our consensus reality.

4

BELIEF SYSTEMS

THE ORGINS OF WHAT I AM WRITING HERE are quite inexplicable. The substance of what I am writing assumes its particular form as if I were a scribe, a reporter recording what comes in from unknown sources and through unknown channels into my mind. At times I am astonished at what appears—it seems not of me nor of mine. I suspect that you've had this experience as well.

There is a variety of possible explanations for this phenomena. First, perhaps like Joan Grant's experiences in *Many Lifetimes,* my present incarnation is writing from memories of previous incarnations. If so, unlike Grant, I do not consciously participate as much as she did in such reincarnations. If states of being from previous incarnations are operative, they are outside my awareness.

Alternatively, this writing may come from entities not of this physical bodily reality, something like what psychic mediums experience. Perhaps forces control my writing from beyond my consciously operating Self.

Perhaps, by an unknown means, an extraterrestrial network of communication feeds the information to me below my levels of awareness. A fourth possibility is that, by a means presently unknown to science and which occur outside my awareness, this writing is created by my bio-computer—my brain, with an "organ of thought" known as "imagination."

Notice that a different belief system regarding where this writing may originate operates in each of the four explanations I just posed. Further, there may be a belief system underlying all four explanations so that they are all are "true." Conversely, all four explanations may be "false." You feel-think the explanations are true or false because your operating systems—your belief systems—have been programmed so that you judge events as "true"—real, or "false"—illusory.

> *That which you do understand will seem "right" to you because "right" is term you use to designate something with which you agree. What you have missed will therefore appear at first to be "wrong". The only way to move forward on this is to ask yourself, "What would happen if everything I thought was wrong, was actually right?" Every great scientist knows about this.*

> —Neal Donald Walsch
> *Conversations with God*

Metabelief Operator

A METABELIEF IS A BELIEF ABOUT BELIEFS THEMSELVES. It is meta—above or on the next level—to the belief under consideration. Thus, a Metabelief Operator is a concept or a function or an agent that operates on, transforms, or introduces changes into belief systems. The Metabelief Operator is outside the belief system that it operates upon. It thinks outside the box—or at least it perceives that there is a box. A Metabelief Operator transforms beliefs, and thereby transforms the perception of reality.

The concept of the Metabelief Operator is useful in understanding the problems posed by the process of our making facsimiles of the various facets of the realities—external and internal. Here the term "operator" is used in the mathematical sense of something that operates on something else to change or transform it.

Your Metabelief Operator can be weak, strong, or nonexistent. If you are quite content with your facsimiles of inner and outer realities, and content with your life as it occurs, there may be little need for a Metabelief Operator. You are content with your beliefs with regards to your family, your business, your religion, your politics—your beliefs work satisfactorily. Your intention is not devoted to questioning and transforming your beliefs. In this case, your Metabelief Operator may be so weak as to be insignificant or functions only to entertain the Self.

> The Metabelief Operator thinks outside the box—or at least it perceives that there is a box.

A crisis, whether physical, mental, or spiritual, can activate a Metabelief Operator in someone who previously did not have such an Operator, or strengthen a weak one. A brush with death, a profound religious experience, a serious accident, a prolonged illness, a financial disaster, a sudden unexpected confrontation with violence, an insightful psychedelic experience— each can generate a need to change beliefs about Self, about external reality, about internal reality. Here the Metabelief Operator may appear and function for a time. It may continue its operations or it may become dormant again.

> *"What is this "I"? You will, on close introspection, find that what you really mean by "I" is the ground-stuff upon which experiences and memories are collected."*
>
> —Erwin Schrodinger

Some people, geniuses of one sort or another, acquire Metabelief Operators quite early in life and continue to use them throughout their lives or they may let them die. Certain artists, scientists, businessmen, and politicians are creative through such Metabelief Operators. Once successful, the need for the Metabelief Operators may become weakened because the beliefs have become satisfying and the need for change has approached zero. Others maintain their Metabelief Operators throughout their lives. Curiosity and interest in challenging and transforming beliefs may be kept alive for decades and be unaffected by aging.

John A Wheeler, the "black hole" physicist, said, "The most important source of energy is the human being and what he believes. I can't think of anything more important than people's views of how man fits into the scheme of the universe."

My personal metabelief system agrees with Wheeler's insight. I spent much of my career studying a "true—as if true" science of belief. As an aside, keep in mind that this whole work is a simulation, even as you are to me and I am to you.

Consensus Reality

CONSENSUS REALITY IS THAT SET OF BELIEFS, which includes assumptions, postulates, interpretations, and simulations, that we have learned are real and true in our culture—society, family, school, and so on. Consensus reality is that which is agreed upon to be real and true by a dyad, a family, a group, a nation, or a group of nations. Some examples are the various human legal structures, like city, county, state, and nation; pictures of realities created by media like newspapers, TV, and radio; financial realities such as those created by banks, taxes, salaries, and wages; and the scientific community's picture of reality.

It is fairly easy to see consensus reality at work in fanatical cults, yet generally difficult to see their operation in our world. Yet, in a sense, we all live in a cult whose members agree upon what is real and unreal, what is right and wrong, good and bad, possible and impossible.

> It is easier to see consensus reality at work in cults, than in our own lives.

In other words, consensus reality is a collection of simulations of internal reality and external reality, with which members of a particular group agree or disagree. Most of our sacred beliefs are actually agreed upon simulations—facsimiles—of reality. Feedback, positive or negative, from lovers, family, as well as with religious, political, and business groups, generates beliefs and disbeliefs in each of us. Once programmed, beliefs are difficult to unearth because we are generally unaware of their powerful existence and influence on our thinking, doing, and feeling. The degree to which we function from this programming is, in a sense, the degree to which we are bio-robots. Humans are distinctly different from robots, however. The human bio-computer can program its Self.

Paper Reality

AN IMPORTANT SUBSET OF THE CONSENSUS REALITIES is paper realities and their counterpart—film and tape realities. In our society we record on paper our contracts, our marriages, our wills, our financial transactions, our news, our history, our thoughts, our opinions. These records determine our actions, our thinking, and our doing to a large extent.

We live up to, or break, our contracts. We marry one person and live together according to our beliefs as to what is a marriage. We make a will in the expectation that its provisions will be carried out after our death. A checking account works because enough people believe in its paper reality. Otherwise a check for a thousand dollars is nothing more than a worthless piece of paper. We believe or disbelieve stories printed in newspapers and shown in TV newscasts. We tend to believe as true that which we read in books and magazines and what we see in motion pictures and on TV. To a large extent, paper reality represents consensus reality. We are immersed in a representation of reality fed to us on paper, on film, on tape.

Speed of Belief Change

THE METABELIEF OPERATOR CAN CHANGE BELIEFS at various rates, from zero to the maximum speed available to the person. During a crisis, the speed of change can be such that the basic beliefs change in a few seconds, hours, or days. By contrast, during slow social change it may take years for beliefs to change.

Consensus reality itself is an aspect of a very large hyper-stable multiple-individual feedback system. It changes slowly in the absence of war, violence, or catastrophe. Metabelief Operators derived from consensus reality reflect this slow rate of change characteristic. In fact, fast belief-changes are generally suspect by the group at large. The person is considered abnormal, far out, diseased, mentally ill, a fanatic, or unstable. They go from operating at the norm to being deviant—different from the group.

The consensus reality feedback loop keeps belief systems stable—static and unchanging; getting out of the consensus reality feedback loop is necessary to speed up belief-change. But how can we do so when we are quite literally immersed in it? There is only one way—go into the void, a place devoid of sensory situation and input-feedback from out there—consensus reality.

Goodness of Fit

YOUR EXPERIENTIAL HERE-AND-NOW REALITY and its directly self-generated simulations may agree or disagree with your paper reality. You may unquestioningly accept the paper, film, and tape realities to become a passive acceptor of the dictates of this aspect of consensus reality. Or you may question these dictates on the basis of your own experience, experiments, insights, and knowledge.

Your Metabelief Operator can operate on the paper-film-tape reality and choose that which has a sufficient goodness-of-fit with your personal simulations of reality. By doing this you develop criteria of what is real and true for you.

4

WHAT IS REAL?

I N MODERN WESTERN SOCIETY there is a vast array of belief systems about the mind and the brain. There are those in religion who believe that the mind is something greater than the computations done by the human bio-computer, which demonstrates an implicit faith that the human mind somehow is connected with a human spirit or soul that transcends the everyday operations of the normal human mind. Such concepts generate a "mind-unlimited" belief .

Belief in an unlimited mind goes back into our dim, distant past, long before written history. It is connected with our religious feelings, with our religious experience, and with the traditional teachings derived from formalized religions. Over the millennia, this belief system has become quite powerful and determines the thinking of millions of people upon this planet.

As we chip away at this major question of existence of Self, as men have chipped away at this question over the millennia, we find that this kind of question and the attempt to answer it have led to new understandings, new mathematics, new sciences, new points of view, and new human activities. It is only recently that a possible alternative to this belief system—mind-limited or contained mind belief—has arisen in science and in medicine.

Defined by Beliefs

IT IS USEFUL TO EXTEND THE USUAL DEFINITION OF REALITY, which we tend to think of as that which is outside the mind, to also include that which is inside the mind. Thus we have an "external reality" and an "internal reality." Our Self is immersed in the internal reality. This is true at all times, even when we are busily engaged in pursuits in the external reality.

What is real and what is true is defined by our beliefs. We interpret what happens to us in light of our beliefs about reality. This means that what we "perceive" is actually a simulation—an interpretation, a model, a fascimile—of the real and of the true. In a given circumstance, we decide what is real and true from experience outside of ourselves—"ex-perience"—and from what we experience inside ourselves—"in-perience".

> Self is always immersed in the internal reality.

Simulations are pictures of reality that we've created from direct in-perience and ex-perience and from the beliefs we've learned, much like a computer creates a picture from data input into it. Even though the data is the same, the picture—the simulation—created varies noticeably from one computer system to another.

Based on Fit

WE BELIEVE SOMETHING TO BE "TRUE AND REAL" in consensus simulations or in simulations of another person when it sufficiently fits our own simulations. Conversely, we judge something as "false and unreal" when it lacks sufficient fit with our personal simulations.

We hold something to be "as if true and real" in the simulations of another when it does not yet fall into our experience but we can see that it is believed as true and real by the other person. Similarly, we hold something to be "as if false and unreal" when we have not yet experienced it, but understand that it is believed to be false and unreal by others. Here our Self is withholding judgment.

We hold something to be "meaningless" when it hasn't as of yet been simulated by our Self or is rejected by our Self through ignorance, inexperience, disbelief, knowledge, insight, or experience. Similarly, we hold something to be "as if meaningless" when others believe it to be meaningless and our Self is withholding judgment.

We use these values to determine what we believe about our states of being. In one state, we experience certain events or simulations as true and real. In another state of being, not overlapping the first one, these same events or simulations can be judged to be as if true and real, to be false and unreal, to be as if false and unreal, to be meaningless, or to be as if meaningless.

For example, when in my flotation tank—my void state—I have a profoundly deep experience of eternal loneliness and unity with the universe. At the time of its occurrence I perceive this ex-perience and in-perience to be true and real. When I return to the busyness of my life with family, colleagues, friends, and co-workers, I am in a state of belief-interlock with these other people. My previous sense of loneliness and unity may now seem only "as if" true and real, or possibly unreal and untrue, or even meaningless. I know it was real and true before, yet now it is only as if real and true, or unreal and un-true, or meaningless. This brings me face to face with the dilemma of what is reality. What is *really* true?

But What is *Really* True?

THIS IS A DIFFICULT QUESTION. Few of our answers are satisfactory. So we hold temporary, to-be-revised notions. Direct here-and-now ex-perience and in-perience may be accepted as true and real.

Memories of past direct here-and-now ex-perience and in-perience are imbedded in simulations and are, therefore, simulations themselves so that they are only as if true and real when replaying what happened. Another possibility is that consensual validation of our ex-perience and in-perience is a mutually agreed-upon simulation.

Non-transferable

YOU MAY BELIEVE A STATE OF BEING TO BE TRUE AND REAL because of direct experience. However, direct here-and-now ex-perience and in-perience is not directly transferable from one mind to another. Each of us generates unique internal simulations of our ex-periences and in-periences that may overlap with the agreed-upon simulation domain, but they are never exactly the same. In a given

We are unaware that we are programmed by consensus reality.

external experience, each of two people ex-periences and in-periences a unique reality derived from their respective simulations. The only overlap is in their descriptions of the ex-periences and in-periences that they share with one another.

We are programmed in destructive directions by consensus reality. And all the while we are unaware that we are thusly programmed. We must experience other realities in order to know that we have choices.

5

CONTAINED MIND

THIS RELATIVELY NEW BELIEF SYSTEM arose from studies of medicine, neurology, neurophysiology, and from the pragmatic way that man and woman treat one another in their everyday relations in the law, in business, and in science. In our everyday relationships we assume that the other people with whom we interact are contained within their physical bodies. We assume that in a person's absence we cannot deal with him or her. When a person is more than a few hundred feet away, in a sense the person is missing—absent. When other people are out of reach of our voice in the external world, or out of reach by telephone, we lose contact with them. At least we cannot make mutual decisions without their actual "presence"—by voice or phone.

We assume that each person is contained within a physical body, and that the person's body must be present or we must use one of our technologies— phone, fax, email, etc.—to communicate with him or her. Out of sight, out of sound, and away from written materials, with no TV set, pragmatically we are each isolated. In short, from our empirical experience, we believe that we and other people are housed by our bodies.

We depend upon the telephone, the written word, the TV image, and the internet to link us with others. Only rarely is it that we have experiences that lead us to wonder if there are possibilities of communication

other than those represented by a direct physical
means, such as seeing the person—a visual image,
speaking by the vocal expression, or by the written
word.

Mind in a Body

EMPIRICAL OBSERVATIONS MADE OVER THE MILLENNIA have
convinced scientists that we humans are confined to a
body and to the brain within that body. When the
brain is damaged, the usual means of communication
can be cut off abruptly and completely. For example,
after a powerful blow to the head, we can see the
person disappear, as it were. The body goes into coma
and we can no longer speak with the person within
that body-brain. That person is said to be unconscious—incapable of communication with others in the
surrounding. The person remains incommunicative
until the coma passes and he or she returns to conscious use of the body and communication is resumed.

On the basis of such observations, modern medicine has assumed that the person is a function of intact
cerebral cortical activity within the central nervous
system. The belief is that the person is limited to a
functioning intact undamaged brain, when in a normal
state and not under anesthesia.

The contained-mind view of humans dominates
our law, such as in *habeas corpus* doctrine, which says
that the body must be present for the law to operate. In
legal proceedings the body is ob-
tained by way of a subpoena. In
psychiatry, the patient must be
present and communication with the
patient is necessary for a diagnosis. In
arriving at a diagnosis, it is assumed
that all the needed information is contained within the
particular body and brain. In the business world, we
deal with other humans in bodies—directly or by
means of our technology—with their particular brains

**Laws are
rooted in the
contained-
mind view.**

and minds contained in those brains. The pragmatic assumption is that if the person is present—in person, by phone, by email—we can make a deal; if the person is not present, we cannot make a deal with that particular person.

Examine the Assumptions

LET US THEN EXAMINE THE ASSUMPTION underlying the contained-mind belief system and see if it can embrace the contradictory phenomena of ordinary everyday waking life interacting with others in physical bodies, and those of dream states, trances, and entheogenic rituals, and religious experiences.

In the contained-mind view, the "mind" is a function of the brain's activities, and of nothing else. The brain is modulated by exchanges with and participations in an external world and the complexity of other humans, animals, and plants as well as by the solidity of the planet.

Let us assume that we can specify all the inputs to a brain and all the outputs from that brain. The inputs to the brain are vision, hearing, tactile sense, position sense, detection of accelerations owing to gravity and motion, the sense of smell, the senses delegated to the regulation of the body itself. The brain's outputs are muscular activities, glandular activities, the intake and output of food, and so forth. In the contained-mind view there are no nonphysical inputs or outputs. The inputs and outputs to and from the brain are those within the body and at the surface of the body.

Non-Waking States

HOW CAN WE ACCOUNT FOR DREAM STATES, trances, entheogenic rituals, and religious experiences if we assume that the mind is contained in the brain, that the mind and the Self are the results of computations of a central nervous system?

For purposes of discussion, let us divide up the Self in various realities into simplified diagrams so that we can grasp some of the variables and parameters in action. In the contained-mind hypothesis, the Self—the Observer-Operator—is the result of the computations of a central nervous system—a brain. In a basic philosophical sense, the Self is the result of those computations. Without the computations, the Self does not exist. Thus, the Self is a program—a Self metaprogram: a self-referential aspect of the computations of that brain. In other words, the Self is the victim, as it were, of that which generates it—the self-referential computations of that brain. In cause and effect terms, the Self is at the effect of the brain's processes.

Unsettling Realization

WHEN A GIVEN OBSERVER REALIZES this source of Self as true, a paranoid reaction of great depth may develop. The person may become hyper-cautious in allowing this knowledge to penetrate awareness. This model, or simulation of Self, may wall the person off from further realizations about the true complexity of the situation. If we assume that the computational processes of a brain are simple, and hence your Self is a result of simple processes, this can induce quite a good deal of fear and paranoia, especially when you realize that "you really are."

> *"Everything you know is in the mind."*
>
> —Peter Russell

Of course, in actuality the computations of a given nervous system the size of ours are immensely complex and we do not really know all of the computations that can take place. To escape the discomfort of thinking that they are the result of computations of a central nervous system, some people will shift to a belief in the unlimited-mind—that their Self is not contained within the computations of the brain. I recommend exploring this possibility to as great a depth as you are capable, with courage, so as to realize your true nature rather than shying off from it because you are afraid.

The computations of a given nervous system the size of ours are immensely complex.

All in The Brain

I WONDERED WHAT WOULD HAPPEN if the body and brain were cut off from sensory input. I studied this in the flotation tank, which isolates the body from inputs and outputs to and from the brain within the body itself insofar as our present science is able to do so. Being in the flotation tank prevents interactions with the external reality and assures a solitudinous body and a solitudinous bio-computer within that body with no further needful exchanges with the external reality.

Under the contained-mind hypothesis there is no way that a person isolated in a flotation tank can communicate with other people. All channels of communication have been eliminated. The contained-mind hypothesis states that there are no means of communication with other people available to the isolated person.

The contained-mind hypothesis postulates that all experiences reported by the people who have been isolated from sensory input as being evidence of what can happen in a contained-mind within a contained-brain. All states, no matter how far out or how far removed from everyday experience are accounted for as having taken place totally within the body and brain of the person.

Testing the Hypothesis

LET US EXAMINE THE CONTAINED-MIND HYPOTHESIS and see if
by using such a belief system we can adequately
account for experiences that belong to the region of the
unlimited-mind, at least theoretically. We must be able
to account for dream phenomena, for experiences with
entheogens, for coma experiences, for deep religious
experiences, and similar phenomena reported by many
hundreds of persons.

I conducted such exploration isolated from sensory
input in a flotation tank, floating in the darkness in the
silence, removed from all known physical means of
communication. I was removed from the external
reality, including clothing, a lighted envi-
External ronment filled with noise, with many
reality signals coming into the body, from many
slowly different sources, including other people. I
faded. took off my clothes, immersed myself in
the tank, floating at the surface in the
darkness and silence—alone. At first I remembered the
immediately preceding external reality fairly vividly.
Slowly these memories disappear. As I abandoned
memories of the external reality, I become preoccupied
with the sensations of the body floating in the blackness and silence and warmth.

After many hours of exposure to such an environment, repeated on a daily schedule, I gradually increased my speed of abandoning the memories of the
external reality and the preoccupation with the floating sensations of the body. I become aware that I am
aware, quite independently, of the body or of the
external reality. I say, in effect, "I know that I am
conscious and functioning without the interlock with
the external world." Preoccupation with remaining
sources of stimulation within the body passes away,
the heart and the respiration and the sensations from
the skin are attenuated to the point where they are
forgotten.

I have gone beyond seeing the differences between open eyes, closed eyes, changing the rate and depth of respiration, playing with my heart and similar activities.

If I were in a disturbed state because of some interaction that has taken place in the external reality, this disturbance may sometimes have gone on for hours. I may have been totally obsessed with a hurt given by another person, or a quarrel. If I remained in the sensory void long enough, this kind of thinking and preoccupation eventually died away.

Other times I fell asleep and went through a long dream sequence and woke up again in the sense that I came back to the body and the brain out of the dream world. With more and more exposure to the tank, I found that between the state of dreaming and the state of being wide awake and conscious of my body there are hundreds, if not thousands, of other states of being in which my consciousness is unimpaired and apparently disconnected from the brain and the body.

Dream States

I OFTEN ENTERED INTO A DREAM STATE in which my body is intact and I walked around upon the very familiar planet in which I existed in the past up to the present. I carried on conversations with people I knew and also with strangers. It was a familiar reality based upon my previous experiences in the external world.

In the contained-mind hypothesis this is explained as a simulation of the Self and the external world—such external reality simulations being part of the internal reality—that were generated within my brain. In such scenarios there is nothing that was surprising, nothing new, nothing unique, nothing bizarre, and I was quite content that this is as I live and have lived in the external reality. In the contained-mind belief system this is a "simulation of Self," of my body and of the external reality of myself, of my body, and of the external reality. For most people this is a safe simulation and expresses a large number of their personal dreams.

Many who have experimented with the flotation tank have reported that such dream experiences have a brilliance and a "reality" far greater than do most dreams. The subject of such an experience seems to be stronger than he or she actually is in normal dreaming states. There is a more intact awareness going on, of voluntariness and a brilliance of the whole scene that is lacking in ordinary dreams.

Strange Self

ALMOST IMPERCEPTIBLY STRANGE extra-terrestrial external realities develop and strange creatures, strange humans not of this planet, appear. My Self and my body remain the same as they were before, in the external world. As I wandered around in the strange extra-terrestrial surroundings I was still my ordinary Self with my ordinary body, but within very strange surroundings.

Sometimes I became a "strange Self" in strange surroundings. My body changed to someone else or something else. I could be looking through the eyes of someone else, realizing that I was doing so. The body that I was inhabiting at that point could have been reading some very peculiar language with which I was unacquainted. The body I was inhabiting could be conversing with another similar strange body. There was a sense of alienness about such experiences of which I was aware.

> Sometimes my body changed to someone else or something else.

The strange Self can also be in an ordinary, known type of external reality and be a stranger among familiar humans. The familiar external reality may seem strange, as if I were a visitor to this planet.

In strange or familiar external realities, there could be transforms of Self in which I lost my body. I could become some other form of body, a point or even a small point existing in a strange or familiar external world. I could travel through the external reality quite freely without known means of locomotion. I could go far above the scene that I was looking at and look down upon it, or I could go down into any aspect of the scene as if I were looking through a microscope, enlarging any aspect of the scene. I could also go outward, as if I were looking through a telescope, and approach galaxies off the face of the planet which I was currently inhabiting.

Sometimes there was a fusion between Self and my surrounds. The surrounds could become liquid and flow in a myriad of colors. At this point the distinctions between Self and the surrounds was lost. I no longer had boundaries; I spread out and became the flowing materials, the flowing energies. There was a loss of the boundaries and the distinctions between Self and the surroundings.

Surroundings can disappear entirely as the Self becomes isolated in a void-like space. The mood of Self can become anything. I could be totally paralyzed with fear or I could be ecstatically blissful and happy, floating in isolation, with no body, with no surroundings, with no external reality—just the reality of Self.

*"If I penetrate to the depths of my existence, the indefinable **am** that is myself in its deepest roots, then through this deep center I pass into the infinite **I am,** which is the very nature of the Almighty."*

—Thomas Merton

All *and* Nothing

I COULD BECOME THE WHOLE UNIVERSE. I become omniscient. I knew everything that happened in the past, was happening in the present, and will happen in the future. I was omniscient, omnipotent, and omnipresent. I could react to this with fear, with joy, with high neutral energy, or with anger.

I could become nothing. There was no Self, no external world, no knowledge, no memory. I become zeroed out. There was nothing left including Self. Awareness and consciousness disappeared.

These are the kinds of experiences that I experienced in dream states. The difference in the tank experience is that there is a heightened awareness, heightened consciousness, and a heightened participation in what is happening.

Dream Experience

WE MUST HYPOTHESIZE that phenomena experienced during internal observation can be accounted for by assuming that it is the result of computations within the central nervous system. In this view, what I experienced in the dream state was the stored simulation or model of past external realities with which I had had experience. Suppose in a particular dream structure of the planetary surface, the people, the buildings, the plants, and so on, are quite familiar. They may be replications of the planetary surface in which I lived. Thus, we arrive at a computed past—a simulated external reality, currently brought out of storage, and computed around the computed Self. In other words, such familiar dream settings can be explained as external reality simulations.

As my dream changed into strange, unique, and new external realities surrounding a familiar Self, I began to see that there were stored, or created anew, strange external realities, apparently not experienced before by my Self. In ordinary parlance I entered the region of "imagination." But what is imagination—actually? I would prefer to say that these are simulations of new external realities generated *de novo* by unknown processes in the brain or by the inherent noise level in the brain that generates new reality appearances. Thus, logically it would seem that within the contained-mind paradigm, simulations of an apparent external reality can be of a familiar stored type or they can be a new unique, created type, which supports the contained-mind view.

During internal reality exploration—imagination, day-dreaming, sleep-dreaming, fantasizing—the body that the Self inhabits can change. I could become someone else—a person I knew or a stranger who I did not yet know, or I could become a strange animal, plant, or other form. Thus, we know that simulations of Self, like those of the external reality, can change to be of a familiar type or a new and unique type.

> I could become the whole universe. I could become nothing.

In dreams and psychedelic experiences, there can be a loss of distinctions between Self, simulations of Self, and simulations of surrounds, so that the simulations and the surroundings become melded. Mixtures of the simulations of Self and of the external reality become blurred and finally disappear. As the boundaries become diffuse, the Self spreads out.

During ecstatic experiences and other altered states of consciousness, simulations of the external reality can disappear completely so that simulations of Self become totally isolated in a domain that has no space, no time, and is eternal. Yet, the Self is still capable of emotion, and can move into any emotional mode. The simulation of Self is still intact, still functioning, and still apparent to Self.

Self-Observation

IN THE FLOTATION TANK, my preferred void space, I had experiences in which simulations of Self disappeared so that Self was everything, spread out, universal, creating everything, creating itself. All simulations of the external reality were gone, all simulations of Self were gone, and there was only a pure consciousness, a pure awareness—consciousness without an object.

On some occasions when in my void space my Self disappeared, everything disappeared. If there was any experience in this state, none of it was brought back when returning to the normal state.

Gather Your Own Data

I DO NOT ESPOUSE THE CONTAINED-MIND MODEL, the leaky-mind, or the universal mind models. My task here is to present alternatives rather than to espouse any one view. I present these considerations to help you in your own researches into your own Self using your own uniquely created "void space." I hope that such models will open up new possibilities for your own direct experience in the void. I hope that this will enlarge your horizons and allow yourself to experience what I have described in a safe way, so that you can be convinced that such things are possible and probable for you.

> As a scientist, my task is to present alternatives, not to espouse any one view.

Many Unknowns

ONE LESSON THAT HAS COME FROM MY EXPERIENCE with sensory void is that the human mind has many unknowns within it. My respect for the mind has moved way beyond where it was when I started the tank research.

Contained & Uncontained Both

It is quite common to believe in both belief systems: the contained-mind and the uncontained-mind. On a particular day of the week you may attend formalized meetings, such as in church on Sunday, or with a religious group in which the uncontained-mind hypothesis operates. During the rest of the week you may operate using the contained-mind belief.

During sleep you leave the consensus way of operating with other persons and enter into regions where other laws and beliefs operate. In hypnotic states and dream states, the laws of the external world may not rule what happens. You can go through experiences with seemingly real persons, either known or unknown. You may be able to control what the other persons say and do. You can melt and flow as if a liquid. You can become a point, a line, or a solid. The laws of the dream states and internal realities do not have the constraints that the external reality has, yet they overlap those of the external reality.

When in alternative states of consciousness, the mind may seem unlimited, to extend out beyond the confines of the brain, of the body. We have all had such experiences within ourselves when asleep and dreaming at night in our beds.

Thus, when asleep and dreaming, the contained-mind becomes an uncontained-mind. Similarly, under the influence of anesthetics, during entheogenic and near-death experiences, during trance, and when in a sensory void, you enter into states of being in which the mind seems to be unlimited and not constrained to the body and brain.

6

Mind Unlimited

I N THE UNCONTAINED-MIND VIEW OF SELF the mind is not contained in a central nervous system. The boundries of the mind, the domains open to the Self, are not limited by the biophysical structure of the brain. Even though most religions and esoteric-mystical schools espouse such belief systems, in this exploration I do not making assumptions similar to or identical with such systems of thought.

Premises

THE UNLIMITED-MIND VIEW STATES THAT, when isolated from all known physical sources of sensory stimulation and communication, there can be sources and signals not yet detectable by modern scientific instruments that can be detected by the Observer-Operator—the Self. These sources and signals can be transformed into information by the central processing system.

Stated another way, there are internally detectable sources of information transmitted directly to the Observer-Operator from unknown sources that are beyond information resulting from central processing of usual sensory input and output signals. Simulations originating in such unknown sources can be transferred directly into the internal reality simulation domain by means that are unknown and not understood by modern science.

While the Observer-Operator is a result of the central processing of the CNS, the Self can exist as a mobile unit or entity that can leave the vicinity of a brain in which it has invested a life interest.

For me, the most satisfactory method is to use the contained-mind system in the normal state and to accept the assumptions of the uncontained-mind "as if true." However, when experiencing these phenomena in the sensory void state the events, processes, and entities are true direct experiences, not "as if true" internal simulations. On return to my normal state, the experiences that were "true and direct" become internal reality simulations—until better evidence of their real existence is furnished by cross-observer validations.

Testing the Fit

TAKING UP EACH OF THESE PREMICES SEPARATELY, we can explicate and examine the unlimited-mind belief system.

Assumption:
Unmeasureable Signals Exist

THE FIRST ASSUMPTION IS THAT THERE EXIST SIGNALS and sources of communication not yet known in science. When physically isolated from sensory input/output, the Observer-Operator may detect unknown signals. This assumption is analogous but not identical to the example of radio waves and atomic particles in 1700 A.D. At that time there was no available instrumental means of detection of either one. Today we can detect such waves and particles, but only with modern scientific instruments.

If there are sources or signals detectable by the Observer-Operator but not detectable by instruments, there is—*as yet*—no acceptable method of experimental scientific verification of such sources and signals.

For example, suppose that psychic mediums actually can receive communications from people no longer living. There is no way to verify this phenomenon with current scientific measuring instruments. To meet scientific protocols, firsthand reports from accepted trained observers must be verified by agreement with the firsthand observations of second, third, and so on to the nth accepted group of trained observers.

If such unknown signals exist, and if they are operative in present observers in the sensory void state, the resulting phenomena in the internal reality and internal reality simulations operate in such a way as to be indistinguishable, at least from our present criteria, from phenomena originating "spontaneously" from central processes and their inherent "noise level," from memory processes, and from Self-programmed phenomena.

If and when instruments can be devised or discovered for detection of such signals—if any, then objective recorded data can be used to separate the at-present indistinguishable phenomena and their origins by means of the simultanously recorded signals.

Assumption:
Self Receives Transmissions

THE SECOND ASSUMPTION STATES that there are unknown kinds of information generated and/or transmitted by unknown means directly to the Self—the Observer-Operator—bypassing the CNS central processing, which results in a kind of "knowing." We've all had this experience.

I know that I know that I know.

This is a mode of communication claimed to exist by mystics, prophets, and gurus in which some suprahuman agency greater than the teacher imparts information directly to them, and possibly through them directly to the disciple. We call these processes inspiration, intuition, direct knowing, and gnosis.

Such processes of direct information transfer may exist. However, from the criteria of acceptable trained observers in modern science, the evidence is remote. Cross-observer validation among trained scientific Observer-Operators is lacking in this critical area.

This assumption does not fit the cybernetic contained-mind belief system. The only evidence for the existence of systems of direct transfer is given by those experiencing phenomena "as if" such systems exist. Only people who believe this assumption give label descriptions "as true," and not "as if true."

What about intuitive "knowing"?

For an untrained Observer-Operator the direct transfer theory is seductive, provocative, and easy because it does not require the disciplines of the scientific model. Untrained observers don't generally insist upon the necessity of validation by cross-observer investigations. On the other hand, the contained-mind beliefs are more satisfactory investigative tools to a scientifically trained observer-operator experiencing the kind of phenomena we've been considering. The contained-mind open to unknown signals and their processing seems more "investigatable," and would seem to have the potential to generate data more easily handled in the scientific domain.

Assumption:
Self Can By-Pass Brain

THE THIRD ASSUMPTION IS THAT the Self can bypass the signal, processing, information, simulation chains of the cybernetic contained-mind system. This is a variant of the direct information transfer theory and implies direct simulation transfer in a similar fashion.

Under this belief system simulations can be transferred directly from supra-human or human sources to us without central nervous system processing. People

espousing this view accept simulations in the internal
reality as real and true events, entities, and processes.
For the believers there are no internal reality simulations, there is only true direct inner experience. These
people accept as "true" rather than "as if true" these
inner phenomena.

Assumption:
Self Not Contained

THE FOURTH ASSUMPTION IS THAT the Self is not contained
in the brain—that the Observer-Operator is free to
move outside the CNS. Several kinds of secondary
assumptions are implied.

The Observer-Operator is within the internal
reality simulations of internal reality and has access to
being programmed by internal reality simulations "as
if" mobile outside the CNS. When the Oberver-Opera-
tor is in one of the assumed states, he or she believes
the internal events are true and also believes they are
not restricted to the internal reality domain. The
Observer-Operator is mobile and not contained in the
CNS processing domaine, and is free of the CNS
constraints. The Observer-Operator is within the
internal reality domain in the CNS processing and is
programmed, with the internal reality simulations, by
unknown outside sources to be "as if" mobile, unconstrained, and free of the CNS processes.

This is essentially the cybernetic belief system
dictating the "as if true" position when the Observer-
Operator is in the normal state. In this view, the
"apparent mobility" is just that—apparent and not
real. The belief in the realness of what one experienced does not continue when in the normal state. This
is the familiar assumption of mystics, yogis, and astral
travel advocates, such as Robert Monroe who described his amazing experiences in *Journeys Out of the
Body*.

This assumption postulates unknown outside programming sources that generate mobility scripts, programs, and realities within the internal reality and simulations of internal reality domains. The Observer-Operator is put through experiences as real by this outside agency. The internal reality context is changed to match the necessary script at each instant.

The experience of the Self as a "programee" can be threatening or enjoyable or quite neutral. Remember the phenomena are taking place within a body and brain isolated from sensory stimulation There is no access here to mysterious forces outside the computational processes of the brain itself. On the other hand, as soon as we no longer believe in the contained-mind model of Self and its apparent limitations, we can move into other belief systems about the same phenomena. My experiences in sensory void were each real enough to believe these assumption.

> The experience of the Self as a "programee" can be threatening or enjoyable or quite neutral.

7

VOID SPACE

WHEN YOU ARE ALONE, LONG ENOUGH, and at low enough levels of physical and human stimulation, the mind turns inward and projects outward its own contents and processes. The brain stays active despite the lowered levels of input and output and actually accumulates surplus energy to extreme degrees.

"You realize beyond all trace of doubt that the world is in you, and not you in the world."

—Nisargadatta Maharaj

Turning inward, examining our minds, their deep and primitive workings, can you see evidence of the actions and inner workings of the positive, pleasure-full start systems and the negative, painful, fear-full stop systems? I believe most of you can unequivocally say, "yes."

A mind—in its pure culture—can see its own true nature, and have an opportunity to see if it can solve its own basic internal self-contained conflicts in order to have a try at changing the unsatisfying parts.

Special Conditions

IN ORDER, HOWEVER, TO SEE SUCH ACTIVITIES IN THE MIND in its pure culture, special conditions are needed. In the profound black darkness of the void space there is no visual stimulus coming to the eyes. In the profound silence there are no sounds coming into the acoustic apparatus. The other sensory systems are at a very low level of stimulation from the external world. You might expect that when there are no incoming sounds or sights that these systems would be absolutely quiet, dark, and empty. This is not so.

In the absence of external excitations coming through the end organs, the perception systems maintain their activity. If excitation does not come from outside, the first explanation is that excitation comes from other parts of the computer—from program storage and from internal body sources of excitations. In the beginning, the self-programmer interprets the resultant filling of these perceptual spaces as coming from outside. In other words, the sources of the excitation are "interpreted" by the Self as if coming from the real world. For certain kinds of persons and personalities this is a very disturbing experience. For them, it implies a kind of telepathy.

Flotation Tanks

AN FLOTATION TANK IS THE IDEAL SPACE to achieve the most complete void experience. The closest approximation to this in an ordinary life is to lie either on a bed in the dark and in the silence or in a bathtub in total darkness and total silence. These are not substitutions for the tank; they are practical compromises for those who do not have a tank available.

Once your mind is freed from the physical environment by this technique, you have the whole range of the human mind available to your self. You are free to exercise your imagination; your thinking capacity is at a maximum. You have available parts of the central nervous system, the cerebellum, for example, that are normally not available for programming by Self under ordinary circumstances. By means of isolation, you are automatically given an expanded province of your mind, in your brain.

Under these circumstances, hallucinations, projections, simulations are all very real. One basic void experience rule is: "No matter what happens do not move." Keep these processes active only in isolation.

Taboo

WE HAVE BEEN TAUGHT FROM BABYHOOD that this kind of phenomenon in a fully conscious individual is forbidden, anti-socia,l and possibly even psychotic. This taboo meta-program was implanted in us during childhood and then continuously reinforced with consensus so that we believe that what is real is real and what is not real is taboo.

To discover who we really are we must examine its rationality or lack of same and proceed in spite of consensus taboos and our anxieties. This taboo is an evasion or a defensive maneuver against seeing the true state of affairs. We can allow ourselves to experience the deeper set of phenomenon of our selves without interfering with natural meta-programs. After achieving this level of freedom from anxiety, we can then go on to the next stages.

What Am I?

"What am I? Am I the bulb that carries the light? Or the light for which the bulb is a vehicle? This body is a vehicle of consciousness. If you can identify with the consciousness, then you can watch this body go, like an old car — there goes the fender. It is expectable. Then gradually the body drops off and consciousness rejoins consciousness, and is no longer in this particular environment."

—Joseph Campbell
as told to Bill Moyers

Providence of the Mind

YOU CAN DISCOVER PROFOUND TRUTHS ABOUT YOUR SELF, about your capabilities through experimenting with your bio-computer in the void state, a state isolated from sensory input. The resulting states of being, of consciousness, teach you the basic truth about your equipment.

The province of the mind is the region of our models, of the alone Self, of memory, of the meta-programs. What of the region, which includes your body and the bodies of others? In the mind, there are no limits.

There is another kind of information in the network of bodies—one's own connected with others for bodily survival, procreation, and creation. But, once again, definite limits are imposed by the bodies of the network housing the minds, the ground on which they rest, the planet's surface. These limits are to be found experientially and experimentally, agreed upon by special minds, and communicated to the network. The results are called *consensus science*.

> In the mind, there are no limits.

The Mystery

GIVEN A SINGLE BODY AND A SINGLE MIND physically isolated and confined in a completely physically-controlled environment in true sensory solitude, by our present sciences can we satisfactorily account for all inputs and all outputs to and from this mind—this bio-computer. Given the properties of the software-mind of such a bio-computer, are we likely to find, discover, or invent inputs-outputs not yet in our consensus science? Does this center of consciousness receive and transmit information by, as of yet, unknown modes of communication? Does this center of consciousness stay in the isolated confined bio-computer? Or can it roam?

Inner Exploration

ALL OF THIS IS A SET OF WORKING HYPOTHESES and as such I must remain quite skeptical of their value except in the operations of achieving certain kinds of states of consciousness and experiencing certain alternate realities. The consensual realities; i.e. those to which our senses tie us—our ears, eyes, gravity sense, position sense, sense of space about us, and space-time continuum, and so on, determine the Self's biophysical bodily survival and also our social prospering in the external social reality.

Therefore, it is well to know what these realities are and respect them and their power. I quickly came to realize that it was best to do my experiments in isolation away from conflicting influences and such persons, and not talk about them while they are going on and only write about them after they are all finished and there is no chance of their being terminated by forces greater than one's Self in the surrounding society.

If you proceed with experiments of your own take the stance here is that everything that you are doing is research, that you are skeptical of the results, and that all of this is a set of working hypotheses to be tested by experiment and experience.

Be Discerning

IN THE VOCABULARY OF A WORKING SCIENTIST, the importance of working hypotheses and skepticism are obvious. I set up a set of working hypotheses of which I was skeptical and examined them in the internal realities with as much scientific objectivity as I could get, after I came out of the belief system and consider what happened. The operational aspect of my working hypothesis was that the working hypotheses become instruction for entering certain states of consciousness and experiencing certain alternate realities.

> All of this is a set of working hypothesis.

Let us consider the realities to which our senses tie us—our ears, eyes, gravity sense, position sense, sense of space about us, and the space-time continuum. These realities are shared between mammals of the human variety because of our ears, eyes, gravity sense, and so forth are stimulated by the same bio-physical ranges of each parameter. Therefore, we can agree on what the external reality is, which each of us is detecting, so it becomes a consensual reality in the sense in which we are using it here.

The Self's bio-physical bodily survival depends upon this external reality, this consensual reality. It is this reality which dictates our social programming and our prospering within a given society in the external social reality. We are a creature which is determined by our senses and by our interactions with those who share the reality of those senses.

In the void space and in sleep, we can escape the interlock of our senses with the external reality; therefore, we can tune in to alternate realities in the absence of the stimuli and in the absence of this kind of sensory interlock.

Discipline

To a considerable extent, the science of realities, whether inner or outer, are each postulated and constructed by the observer. If, in his simulations—in his models, his ideas, his thinking machinery as modified by contact with the universe—he sees the way through the discipline of the external realities to the discipline of the internal realities, then a person can become complete, instead of a half-person—an inner person or an outer person.

When this is accomplished, you find depths dimly seen in your daily state of consciousness. You find the programs that operate you—the positive and the negative, rewarding and punishing activities deeply imbedded within yourself. Many men and women before us knew these experiences.

No Alibis

THE COGENCY AND URGENCY OF FINDING and understanding the internal origins and substrata of rewarding and punishing systems are obvious to many persons. But you must avoid taking too seriously that which you have within yourself and that is found so clearly by persons in sensory isolation. I encountered projections of negative and of positive motivations and powerful projections that seemed to come, acting "as if," from other persons—external reality—but actually originating inside my own Self.

An advantage of such Self exploration in sensory isolation as compared to other kinds of situations is that there are no real present excuses to blame for the emotional storms of love and hate, the fantastic beliefs, or the mental projections which can and do occur. Alone with one's God there are no alibis.

In sensory isolation the evidence of the truth of the existence of your own projections becomes so obvious as to be inescapable and humbling. Outside in external reality you use ingenious and subtle techniques well-known to psychoanalysts and psychotherapists to escape this realization.

The human mind is the only province in science in which that which is assumed to be true either is true—or becomes true. Holding a useful and successful set of basic beliefs is a sublime and dangerous faculty. Truths about the rewards and punishments in the Self is sublime, sometimes satisfying, and sometimes punishing—but never dull or monotonous. To find your Self to be more ego-philic than ego-phobic is, of itself, an advantage to increasing your fun and that of those persons closet to you. By careful and continuous nurturing you can achieve the command to "love thy neighbor as thyself," but only after learning how to increase the love for thyself.

> Alone with one's God there are no alibis.

The experience of higher states of consciousness—alternate realities—is the only way to escape our brain's destructive programming implanted in us as children by a disgruntled karmic history. Newborns are connected to the divine war as the result of our programmed disconnection from divine sources.

Unique Self

ONE FACT WHICH MUST BE APPRECIATED for applying this theory is the essential individual uniqueness of each of our minds, of each of our brains. It is no easy work to analyze your Self or someone else's. This theory is not, and cannot be, a miracle key to a given human mind. It is devilishly hard work digging up the basic facts—the basic programs and meta-programs—controlling each mind from within itself. Yet, understanding the basic programming of a mind is essential for rewriting its programs, to change its poor operations into better ones.

> One fact which must be appreciated is the essential individual uniqueness of each of our minds—of each of our brains.

Investigation of Self is not easy or fast. Built-in prejudices, biases, repressions, and denials fight against understanding. Unconscious programming automatically controls our behavior. Eventually humans may be able to progress farther. It could take several generations.

Why Void?

AT CERTAIN TIMES I FOUND IT ESSENTIAL to be able to relax completely irrespective of anything that is going on in the environment. Sometimes I'd wake up in the middle of the night with an idea that I wanted to work out, so rather than disturb my wife, I'd go to my void space—my sensory flotation tank—and work out the idea at great length and in fine detail. I was then able to put it down on paper or to dictate it in the morning.

When I was worn-out during the day, instead of taking a long nap, I'd seek total sensory isolation for a half an hour. This not only allowed me to deprogram that which had been going on previously, but permitted me as well to recharge my biological battery in the midst of busy activities. I found that the sensory isolation experience was an absolute necessity in order to recover during the day quickly and easily from overloads brought about by too much activity, too much exchange with other people, too much travel.

For example, I was shoveling gravel and installing a new antenna system from seven o'clock in the morning till five in the afternoon. I was physically worn-out—in that delightful state of muscle fatigue but so worn-out that there was an inability to remember where I had left the tools. I had a pressing engagement at 6:30 that evening—a rather important conference with several people. Somehow I had to recharge the brain and the body.

> When worn-out, instead of taking a nap, I'd seek total isolation for a half an hour.

I went into the void space of my flotation tank and allowed the activities of the day to gradually disappear from my mind. As the day's residues slowly but surely disappeared, I went into a place in which the blackness, the silence, and the floating were the only contents in my consciousness. I did not go to sleep, but entered an abstracted state where there was no body, no external reality, only the floating, the darkness, and the silence. By objective outside time, I did this for only thirty minutes. The inside time in the internal reality disappeared. I came out of the void completely refreshed, full of energy, and ready for anything that was needed.

"The athlete who is in championship form has a quiet place and it is out of that that his action comes. If he's all in the action field, he's not performing properly. There's a center out of which you act. Unless this center is found you are torn apart, tension comes. Nirvana is a psychological state of mind. It is not a place like heaven. It's not something that's not here. It is here in the middle of the turmoil, the whirlpool of life's conditions. Nirvana is the condition that comes when you are not compelled by desire, or by fear, or by social commitments— when you hold your center and act out of there."

—Joseph Campbell
as told to Bill Moyers

This alternation of high mental and physical activity with recovery in sensory void was the key to my particular creativity. The flotation environment is a relaxing, refreshing, sage place where I recovered my energy. I found that in a busy day, a half-hour break in sensory isolation restored energy to the mind and the body. Gardening, hiking, desk work, writing, dictating, typing—each of these activities takes a toll of available energy. Sensory isolation, especially in the flotation tank, restored my free, available energy.

Most people are able to achieve such restoration early on in their void experiences. With practice, it becomes easier to relax more of your body and your mind. With experience, the benefits arrive more easily and faster. At first an hour may be used; later, in a series, twenty minutes may suffice. Most people feel a renewed clarity of perception similar to awaking after a good night's sleep.

The void state is a resting place and a "think tank" for working out problems and can be of considerable benefit. For those who wish to penetrate the deep Self, pursue self-analysis, use the deeper meditations, explore reality in greater depth, the void state a useful tool. It allows the inner realities to be penetrated as deeply as you are capable as external realty is minimized almost to zero when in the darkness and silence of the void state.

By integrating, organizing, meditating on void versus non-void experience, you discover for yourself the uses of this restful tool in your own planet-side trip.

Alone with one's God,
there are no alibis.
There is no goat on
which to project the
negative, nor a lover
on which to project
the positive.

8

FROM HERE TO THE FARTHEST ZERO

N ORDER TO BECOME, to be, to move,
Imagine leaving here, going to a cliff above the sea.
Watch the sea,
Dive into the air, down into the sea.
Dive deep toward the bottom.
Feel the entities in the sea, in the cool-darkness, the
    pressure.
Listen and communicate with them.
They know the secret way of escape from here.
Escape into other places far from this planet.
Move up from the sea's depths.
Slant up through the dark cold, up to the warmth.
Move out of the sea's surface, into light.
Travel through the earth's air space, out.
Accelerate toward our star, the sun.
Feel its radiance increase, its energy.
This energy started, maintains us, is us.
Enter the sun's flaming self, be its light,
Be its energy, share the star as you.
Be the sun, shining into space.
Move away on its energy, become greater that this star.
Spread as its light in all directions.
Fill the universe with thee, be the universe.
Be all the stars, the galaxies are your body.
Be the empty space spread self to infinity.
Be the creative potential in the empty spaces.
Be the potential, infinite in the absolute zero of nothing.

9

ENTERING ALTERNATE REALITIES

Wheeler's hyper-space is also known as a "non-local reality." Each of a pair of photons coming from an atom knows immediately what the other is doing, no matter how far away from each other they are. You can assume the existence of tachyons—faster-than-light-particles that carry messages—but I prefer Bell's theorem solution to the Einstein-Podolski-Rosen experiment, which illustrated a connectedness between particles in two different places. According to Bell's theorem, hyper-space is a region of hidden variable in which all realities are represented at a single point and in which there is no need for messages to travel.

The alternate realities that we are considering here seem to be equivalent to those given in quantum mechanical theory. In order to straighten out some of the paradoxes of quantum mechanical theory, there is a postulation of "the region of hidden variables" or of hyperspace or of alternate realities.

The alternate realities are all connected into hyperspace and to the consensual reality in which we are all immersed. With proper programming within the brain itself, it is possible to move into hyperspace and into some of the alternate realities.

Most of the experiences are "beyond the screen of words." Hence, it is very difficult to bring back adequate descriptions, adequate maps of the alternate realities themselves. A few can be specified by certain kinds of participant observers. Others are beyond the description even of the experts. I began a map of these unordinary realities.

Domain Maps

YOU CAN NOT BE TOO SURE of exactly which of a set of alternate realities you may enter. Robert Monroe encountered a similar experience in his out-of-body adventures, which he described in his book, *Journeys Out of the Body*. He never knew where he was going until he got there. Programming is not yet totally under the control of our Operators and participant Observers. There seem to be intelligences far beyond human, which are involved in our programming—in ways we are yet to discover.

I discovered a hole in the universe though which I gradually learned to see.

I have created domain maps of internal realities that are useful for those of you who seek to change your belief systems in order to develop a more flexible and powerful set of meta-beliefs and meta-belief operators.

During deep penetrations into the internal realities domain, I came upon phenomena not usually experienced in my everyday life. In the dark silence of the void, I lost awareness of my physical surroundings, my body, external reality simulations, my internal reality, my internal reality simulations, my identity—simulation of my Self, myself as a unique individual Self, my humanness, and even the planet and its external realities.

Ease of entering these alternate states is determined by the limitations of programming and meta-programming in your bio-computer. It is a function of the level of self meta-programming, of super-self meta-programming, and of non-self Super intelligence programming that can occur. The unique configuration

of these three factors is part of the holonomic programming, including changing molecular configuration of
brains.

Factors Influencing Ease of Entering Alternative Realities

1) Level of Self Meta-Programming

2) Level of Super-Self Meta-Programming

3) Non-Self Super Intelligence Programming
   potential

Methodology in mapping your exploration is
essential—especially if it is to be "scientific." Audio
taped reports of experiences in the void made during
the experience or immediately following it is a proven
method of recording data. If booster substances are
used, such as alcohol or entheogenic plants, then these
should be carefully logged. People often find indi-
vidualized portals into alternative realities with this
participation-observing approach—which is a traditional scientific approach. It is the essential method for
mapping new spaces—and for finding your way back
from the wilderness.

Keep a Journal

JOURNALING IS A TRADITIONAL RECORD-KEEPING METHOD.
Basically it is a diary of your experience in the void but
done with more discipline. It is important to log the
conditions of each venture into the void, which includes all events surrounding the experience including
substances use as mentioned above, but also your
mental state—your in-perience at the onset. Make note
of your mood state, feelings, expectations, and fears.
Include the state of your well-being. How rested are
you? Note your level of hunger and the last time you
ate, and so forth.

After many void experiences, it is illuminating to read over your journal, looking for patterns. Write summaries of the patterns you notice and your analysis of what they may indicate.

Automatic Programs

WHEN EXPLORING ALTERNATIVE REALMS it helps to have automatic programs, which detect certain undesirable qualities as you start to enter it and key into saying, "No, don't go into that state." Each of us has a few seconds of natural entry that occur as falling asleep, or when drunk,

> The programming challenge is to enlarge the few seconds of natural entry into minutes, then hours.

or when totally fatigued but must keep going, or when making love, and so on. The programming challenge is to enlarge those few seconds into minutes, then hours.

The goal is to get control of the transition from one reality to another, from awake to asleep, rational to erotic, so that you can widen the narrow time slot that you begin with into a full fledged portal—one you can enter at will.

10

CONVERSATION WITH THREE BEINGS

W HEN I BEGAN MY EXPERIMENTS in the isolation tank I didn't know that I was about to discovered a hole in the universe through which gradually I learned to see into another reality. It scared me. I didn't know about alternate realities at that time, yet I was experiencing them right and left in the tank.

I experienced states in which I contacted the creators of the universe, as well as the local creative controllers—the Earth Coincidence Control Office, or ECCO. During these experiments I discovered "Super Intelligences" that are generally reasonable, yet at the same time can be quite ruthless in teaching, whether the Observer likes it or not. They're the ones who run the earth and program us, though we are not aware of it. When I asked them, "What's your major program?" they answered, "To make you people evolve to the next levels, to teach you, to kick you in the pants when necessary."

I'm reporting the experience here as if words had been used, as if the two Beings had spoken to me in English, as if I had become the Third Being.

First Encounter

THE CONFERENCE OF THE THREE BEINGS TOOK PLACE in a dimensionless space, the spaceless set of dimensions somewhere near the third planet of a small solar system dominated by a type-G star. The organization which they represented I would later call the Earth Coincidence Control Office (ECCO).

The First Being: *"We are meeting at this particular space-time juncture in order to review the evolution of a vehicle that we control on the planet Earth. He is at another transition point in his training. We need to review what he has done, what he is thinking, what his motivations are. We must determine what the future of his mission can be within the evolutionary speed limit allowed the humans on that planet."*

Second Being: *"You, the First Being, and I, the Second Being, have been controlling the coordination of coincidences of this human agent on Earth. I feel it is important that we state all of this very clearly for the benefit of the Third Being, who has been responsible for that human-agent. It is important that he not exceed the evolutionary speed limit at this particular time; however, we realize that there is a certain discrepancy existing among the humans, that their evolution is proceeding extremely rapidly in certain areas and is going backward in others.*

"It is the purpose of this conference among the three of us to make sure that the Third Being controls him so that he stays within certain well-defined limits and avoids the kinds of catastrophes certain other agents of ours have experienced on that planet. Let us listen to the report of the Being who has been in charge of the vehicle on the planet Earth."

Third Being: *"Currently my agent is in a quandary. I need this conference to know in what direction he is to move next. The vehicle that he inhabits is now in a deep trance state and is willing to share with us the sources of this quandary.*

"As you both know he has a carefully constructed cover story in which he has invested a good deal of time, effort, and training. All three of us are well acquainted with the rather arduous steps that he has been taking in his human form. There have been many times when he has lost contact with me, has repressed his knowledge of me, and has had to be guided through his unconscious mind. There were times when he had too much knowledge of me, necessitating repression so that he could continue to function as an acceptable human being in the society in which he lives. His main worry at times was being made persona non grata *by his fellow humans in various fields of endeavor.*

"He went through a process which humans call psychoanalysis. Psychoanalysis to us is a means of educating humans in how to remain human, at the same time keeping sufficient independence of that state so as to be aware of our existence. Psychoanalysis also furnishes the human agents with the current rationalizations and basic assumptions upon which humans operate. It helps them develop their cover story so that they will not reveal our existence or our influence. It allows them to reconstruct their past history and understand it in terms of the present human society.

"In the area of self-awareness, his awareness of me—of his deeper self—our human agent is on the threshold of recognizing us and our influence on him.

"In his brain research he has discovered the difference between small brains (monkeys) and large brains (human and dolphin). He has realized that in order to do research on the brain and the mind, he must work in an institution which he himself controls, insofar as is possible in the current human reality. He sees that human society interacts with him in a way that allows certain areas of research and not others. He realizes that the laboratory work in relation to the isolation tank is difficult to support. He has learned that the brain work can be supported openly and that the tank work must be done covertly. As long as the tank work was done in solitude, he was unimpeded in the directions in which he could carry it.

"He is becoming aware of the political and social realities of what he is doing. His mission to thoroughly investigate the brain with thousands of electrodes and with feedback between his own brain and its recorded activity has implications which he knows he cannot reveal at the present state of development of the human species. His analyst taught him to look more critically at this particular aspect of his mission. His work for the last five years has been in the direction of perfecting electrodes so that he can use them safely in his own brain. He found on monkeys and dolphins that this was not a safe procedure. The brain sections revealed damage

*along every electrode track to the extent that he
would not wish to insert electrodes into himself
or another human.*

*"From his interactions with the government
agency in which he has worked, he finally
realizes that the isolation tank gives him more
information in more dimensions than can be
absorbed by those in control.*

*"He now wishes to abandon the study of
electrodes. They are too damaging to brains. He
wants to pursue other methods, not including
brain electrodes or damage to either his own
brain or monkey or dolphin brains.*

*"His work to date with dolphins has con-
vinced him that they are quite as intelligent,
quite as ethical, quite as sentient as humans."*

Second Being: *"What are his basic beliefs about
the existence of the Third Being and about us?"*

Third Being: *"He is oscillating between two
belief systems. In the first he believes that the
mind is the computational software of the brain,
that the brain evolved on the planet Earth from
the forebears of Man and generated Man's
consciousness. In the second system, he believes
in us. This belief is contaminated by his childhood faith in the soul.*

*"He has yet to develop a pure, integrated
view of the mind as an entity not contained in
the brain. He has yet to give up the view that
the brain contains a computed mind plus access
to us through means at present unknown on the*

planet Earth. When he is in the isolation tank for a sufficient period of time, the second belief system begins to take over. When he is in the laboratory or dealing with the realities of the support of his research, the contained-mind belief system takes over."

Second Being: *"I would like to suggest that we arrange for his education in more profound ways. He still needs to penetrate into his own mind deeply in the areas of interest to us."*

Third Being: *"He is making progress in that direction. Currently his plans are to establish his own laboratory in an isolated location in the Virgin Islands in the Caribbean Sea for research with intact dolphins."*

First Being: *"When he leaves the government and goes to the Virgin Islands, I suggest that we control the coincidences in the direction of encouraging the dolphin research. He has much to learn about the Beings known as dolphins.*

"We must also control the coincidences in regard to his seeking a female partner for a dyad. He has much to learn here, not all of which can be taught him without some pain. He is not yet in sympathy with the female mind among humans on his planet. He projects too much of himself, not realizing that there are two universes of humans, male and female. Nor is he aware that in the human social reality there are many substructures of the male-female relationship. In his first marriage he was more

or less detached. He must now learn to attack negatively to find the parameters of balance in the dyadic domain."

Second Being: *"It is felt that coincidences must be regulated to help him continue the isolation work under better circumstances."*

Third Being: *"We must continue our cover of our existence in his mind: if he is too aware of us at his current stage of training, he will be unable to operate in the human realities. I suggest that we temporarily cut off his awareness of us until later, when he is better prepared to deal with our existence."*

First Being: *"Let us adjourn this conference and meet at some future time in regard to our business with this agent."*

Required Caution

I realized the very narrow framework in which this material must be written in order to be published, bought, read, and understood by a sufficient number of people to carry out the necessities of the mission assigned to me.

I am not here, even though you may project a simulation of me. As I write this I am projecting my simulation of you. Please don't take it personally.

If you embark upon this exploration of realities, entered through the void, you must be ready to experience pain, fear, and anger in response to frustrations induced by these Super Intelligences.

As I sat in my office, the first gray light of dawn was appearing. As I considered what to write, the sun came up and shone upon my back. I felt my body, I felt the reality of my office, I felt the reality of what had happened to me in the void. My bio-computer began to generate objections to writing it down. I thought, "Was it all merely a dream, an imaginary situation, a science-fiction script?"

I thought through many alternatives, considering them all, and decided to write, as best I could, the inner reality as an actual happening insofar as I was allowed to report it. Then I reviewed my theory of the contained versus the uncontained mind and began my quest again.

11

WHAT I FOUND IN THE VOID

WHEN IN MY VOID STATE—the flotation tank—I become aware of new experience and in-perience. I discovered that the apparent external reality was actually a tapestry of simulations. What stunned me at first was the discovery that our simulations are penetrable by means other than those we experience or believe to be real by external our consensus reality.

When I cut off sensory input I become aware that my Self was programmed by program systems I had not been aware of in my daily external reality. I became aware that entities other than my Self could interact with me in the void by means not present in our currently recognized consensus science.

I discovered that I am something and someone far greater than my simulation of my Self. I became so deeply interlocked with something far greater than humanness that my Self disappeared as an individual human being and I unified with a "network" of creation. In the void state, I found that my Self could move out of my body to any where, any time, any form. I have not been the only explorer of these states. Experiences of such phenomena found in the void state have been recounted by other people as well.

Projection and Beyond

CONTENT EXPERIENCED UNDER VOID STATE conditions lacks strong reality clues because externally real displays are not furnished in inner space and alternative realities. Stimulation from the reality outside does not pattern the displays on my bio-computer screen, which includes the fantasies, the projections, or the imaginations—whatever they "really" are. Therefore, I conclude that the projections that occur must be from those systems at the next inward level from the operations of the perception apparatus devoted to external reality.

> I discovered that I am something and someone far greater than my simulation of my Self.

We can project living images external reality equivalents—in the visual space or blackness— absence of external reality images. We can project definite sounds—as if external reality— such as voices. Or we can project silence-absence of sound as we know it in the external reality. We can project our body image, such as flexing our muscles and joints to reassure us that the image is functioning with real feedback. Or we can have a perception of a lack of the body image which is the negative logical alternative to the body image itself.

When we abandon the use of projection of external reality equivalents, new phenomena appear. Thought and feeling take over the spaces formerly occupied by projected external reality equivalents. In the psychiatric terminology, we would say that ego expands to fill the subjectively appreciated inner universe. "Infinity" similar to that in the usual real visual space is also involved. I felt that my Self extended infinitely out in all directions. The Self was still centered at one place but its boundaries have disappeared and it moved out in all directions and extended to fill the limits of the universe as far as I knew them.

One explanation of the phenomenon is that I filled the perception spaces with programs, meta-programs, and self meta-programs which were modified in the inner perception into "as if" equivalents. Words can not describe the transformation into this special mental state. To be appreciated it must be experienced directly. In ordinary experience there are dreams which have something of this quality and show this kind of phenomenon. In sensory isolation, when making deep penetrations into the internal realities domain, I often came upon phenomena not usually experienced in everyday life as we know it in our culture.

Various evasions can take place. I could "imagine" that I was traveling through the real universe past suns and galaxies. I could "imagine" that I was communicating with other beings in other universes. However, scientifically speaking, it is fairly obvious that I was not doing any of these things and that my basic beliefs determined what I experienced in the void state. Therefore the ordinary perception spaces have become filled with cognition and conation processes. This seems to be a more reasonable point of view to take than the oceanic feeling of being at oneness with the universe and of as fusing with the Universal Mind as reported in the literature by others for these phenomena. These states, which I call direct perceptions of reality, are my thoughts and feelings expanding into the circuitry in my bio-computer which is usually occupied by perception of external reality in every mode, including vision, audition, etc.

> You may try your usual evasions of Self.

Similarly you may try your usual evasions of Self. For example, you may carry out multiple tape-loop dances, yet you cannot escape the fact that you are alone. Fairly quickly you will find out if you are Self-confident or Self-phobic.

Observing

THE VOID SPACE IS A BEAUTIFUL PLACE to study your hunger and your reactions to hunger. If you have fasted, say for twelve hours, and then go into the void early in the morning, you will probably notice that you are not hungry in the beginning. Hunger may or may not develop at some point during the subsequent hour or two. If this happens, stay in isolation and monitor the hunger and you will find that it comes and goes. At about the point that you're likely to feel an almost overwhelming urge to get out of your void space to eat, the hunger will suddenly disappear. Try this experiment and see if this applies to you.

13

CREATING YOUR VOID SPACE

For those who do meditation, creating a void space is a definite aid. While meditating, sitting cross-legged or on a chair, or lying in a bed, you can examine the environment, the sounds coming from the environment, and whatever light patterns are shifting around in that environment. Slowly but surely during the meditation, you can inhibit the responses of these patterns of stimulation and get deep down inside your mind. It turns out that the sensory isolation environment—the void space—does for you what you must do inside your own mind-body when meditating in the usual environment.

It is not necessary to have any expectations upon entering your void space. You may go there for a rest, to get away from the busyness of your life for an hour or two; you may have a problem in the middle of the night in which case your void space, rather than a bed, is more suited to relax your muscles, provide the rest that you need physically, and at the same time allow mental operations to continue toward solving the problem.

Crutch Programs

Certain people take any method, tank or drugs or whatever, and become addicted to it as a "crutch." I call these "crutch programs." If you allow the void space to become a crutch program, you can change your state of consciousness quite readily to anything that you desire—in the void, but you cannot do this under other circumstances. This is a sure sign of a crutch program operating. An exclusive necessity of any outside aid for a given state of consciousness is defined as a crutch program.

We can learn with the aid of the flotation tank or other void space to do things with our state of being, our consciousness. We can practice what we learn in the void outside of it under other circumstances, say, lying on a bed in isolation and solitude, or under whatever other circumstances you wish to work with. For this point of view a good training is to go into a cave, or into the desert, and be alone in pure solitude and examine some of these things. **You can tune your internal eyes.** Under these other circumstances we are interlocked with the environment, but without the demanding, attaching "people effect." Through this we can generalize our skills. Finally you can learn to be able to close your eyes in the middle of a conference for a period of a minute or two and change your state of being, of consciousness, as you desire.

I can open my eyes in this reality and dimly see an alternate reality, then close my eyes, and the alternate reality picks up. You can tune your internal eyes. It is a little like when you merge your two eyes' images and a hologram-like image appears. Perhaps someday, if we learn about the type of radiation coming through our eyes, we will be able to simulate the experience with a hallucinatory movie camera—an alternate reality camera.

Essential Conditions

CERTAIN CONDITIONS ARE NECESSARY for achieving the void state. Most importantly, you must be alone. Sensory input must be reduced as much as possible. Avoid expectations.

Be Alone

MOST OF THE TIME WE ARE NOT ALONE. We are immersed in an organized human society. The internal origins of our motivations are obscured in a medley of organized background noses, sights, clothing, housing, transport, schedules, and deluges of information demanding replies and action. Thus solitude is the first requirement of readiness to enter the void. You must be freed of persons and people.

To enter the void space, you must be alone, without a lover to exchange the positive, and without a human sacrificial goat to load with the negative. When you are alone long enough in surroundings which are the same, our internal mental workings reveal their basic character rather quickly, in a few hours.

Other Persons

THE MOST ACTIVE, ATTACHING, AND DEMANDING SOURCE of stimulation is another person or group of persons. To free yourself from this imposing source you must go into the solitude of the void space. In a sense, there is no way to achieve the full effects of solitude without allowing sufficient time to pass in the void between your last contact with a person or persons and your current aloneness in a void situation. The leftover programming from contacts with others can be considered as a continuing invasion of your solitude, which is easily seen after being in a void space for an extended period of time.

> Other people are an active, attaching, demanding source of stimulation.

In accounts of people who have been in solitude in the Arctic or alone on small boats sailing across the ocean, there is a period of many days in which the effects of the contacts with humans still persist and until they gradually die out. In a sense, we must devise programs or meta-programs to help attenuate the effects of the leftover programming and meta-programming of the other people.

Turn Off Sensory Input

SAMENESS AND EVENESS ARE ABSOLUTELY NECESSARY for examining your Self and its programming. You must be freed of sources of information from our residual surroundings, animate and inanimate. This can be accomplished by dramatically reducing sensory input. As a corollary, to free yourself from external influence you must have maximum attenuation of physiological and physical stimuli of reactions and exchanges with surroundings, including gravity and temperature's powerful demands.

Light & Visual Images

WE ARE SIGHTED ANIMALS. A very large fraction of our cerebral cortex is given over to visual processing, in terms of perception, central data processing, and outputs from this region. Our memory and our language are closely allied to our visual experience.

We say, for example, "I picture your face when you are not here." We do not say, "I hear your face when you are not here." A dolphin, on the other hand, might communicate, "I hear your face," but a human says, "I see your face." We also use words such as "I imagine," or "I envision," which have to do with visual operations and their analogues in thinking processes.

Visual Displays

ENTERING THE VOID STATE REQUIRES FREEDOM from all light stimulation, including non-patterned light stimulation. This is accomplished by going into a completely blacked-out space—a dark room—in which there are no sources of light whatsoever. Even so, isolation from the "light" is not complete. There are persisting central process visual activities, which you can observe by opening your eyes in the dark and "looking." You may see peculiar cloud-like phenomena, or you may see points of light, flashes of lightning, and so on, depending upon your present state. This occurs be-

———————————— cause the visual system, isolated,

In void space maintains its activity in a "visual work we have display" mode.

"waking dreams"   In special states of being, when in the dark.   in a completely black room, you can see light levels comparable to a well-lighted room, which is commonly called "hallucination." I prefer the more useful and operational term "visual display."

Visual displays are not necessarily produced directly by the Self meta-programmer. Levels of the bio-computer below your awareness generate visual displays, some of which are random in appearance or "noisy" and some of which are well-organized.

For certain neuro-physiological and philosophic reasons, visual displays are what you actually see when in a well-lighted room. It seems strange when it occurs in a dark room because you are not used to your bio-computer producing visual displays in the dark, even though it is a very natural process. We can dream, for instance, in full Technicolor in complete darkness with our eyes closed. In void space work we, as it were, have "waking dreams" in the dark and see fully lighted three-dimensional colored objects without benefit of light. Presumably these visual displays are produced from the storage mechanisms of the human bio-computer.

Sound

SIMILAR TO THE VISUAL SPHERE, the acoustic sphere in the void is filled with information from your bio-computer. There is an inherent noise level within the central nervous system and within the end hearing organs. There is a very rich internal set of sounds, which we call sonic displays analogous to the visual displays, which the bio-computer and its end organs create *de novo*. When in the void space, some people hear very high-pitched whistles, others hear popping sounds like bacon frying, or rumblings and hissings.

Additionally, there are intra-body sources of sound, such as the respiration and the heart. You can attenuate these somewhat by careful body position and careful breathing. Sometimes you can hear gut sounds as well. As more time and more void sessions are experienced, these sounds tend to disappear from the awareness domain.

Hard to Eliminate

WHILE LIGHT IS ONE OF THE EASIEST of the stimulation modes of energy to eliminate from your environment, sound is not so easily eliminated because is transmitted through solids, through liquids, and through gases. You can eliminate, or at least attenuate, airborne sounds most easily by interposing a solid or liquid barrier between your ears and the sound sources. The mass per unit area and the sound velocity in the material interposed between the sound source and the ears determine how effectively the barrier will attenuate sound.

An air-water interface is excellent for turning most of the sound around to prevent it from penetrating into the water from the air. The acoustic mismatch here is 5000:1 This is a better barrier than, say, a steel plate underwater, which is only 500:1, by the way. Stated another way, when you are immersed in water, airborne sounds hitting the water will be reflected in the ratio of 5000:1 which means that only 1 part of 5000 of the energy of the sound that hits the water will be transmitted to the water.

> Sound is transmitted through solids, through liquids, and through gases.

Sound can be significantly attenuated in the flotation tank by immersing your eardrums in the water. This is one of the reasons that it is designed such that you float a little below the surface, so that your ears are fully immersed, while your mouth and nose are above the water level. Water-loaded eardrums are sharply reduced by 30 to 40 decibels—sensitivity to airborne sound. Tanks with dense walls made of lead, steel, or other metal are extremely effective as are concrete, rock, in reflecting sound to further attenuate how much sound can be transmitted into the water.

Immersing your eardrums in water can attenuate sound transmission.

Sound in Dry Void

FOR DRY VOID SPACES SUCH AS A ROOM OR BOX, "sound mirrors" can be used for maximum sound reflection way from the person in the void space. In lieu of sound mirrors you can use absorber "sound-black" materials such as acoustic tile, old-fashioned cardboard egg cartons, and similar materials. These materials operate in a very different way and are less effective. Sound-black materials set up interference patterns among the sound waves so that they destroy one another when the sound enters into the fibrous structure. The friction of the sound traveling within very narrow passageways absorbs the energy. This absorption process is never complete and the transmitted component of the residual reflected component can be considerably higher that the reflected component itself. In physics we say, "an open window absorbs 100 percent of the sound." This is used as the standard of absorption, i.e., it is an instance where there is no reflected component; the sound escapes rather than being merely partially absorbed.

Other sources of sound are those coming through the solids and the liquids, such as through rigid piping in the walls of the dark room or flotation tank. In the tank these sources can be extremely powerful. Liquid or solid conducted sound is difficult to attenuate before it gets into the tank. Generally it's best to use flexible tubing in the water or air supplies leading to tanks so that the tubing will not transmit much sound through its solid structure. For void spaces in dry rooms and boxes, using baffling and absorbing materials in the acoustic pathways can attenuate sound from the liquid and air sources.

Floor-Borne Sound

SOUND TRANSMITTED FROM OUTSIDE SOURCES TO the flotation tank through, say, a concrete floor, has to be attenuated also, which can be done by suspending the tank or void box on the top of the materials, that give an acoustic mismatch between the tank and the floor. In other words, if the tank is built of plywood and it rests directly on a concrete floor, there will be almost 100 percent sound transmission.

These sounds can be attenuated by inserting an acoustic filter between the tank bottom and the floor. You might put and place the tank or void box on top of a steel plate between thick rubber sheets, for example. Another way to attenuate floor-borne sounds is to weave a garden hose back and forth in a spiral or a sine-wave fashion under the flotation tank or dry void space. The garden hose arrangement has several advantages. It gives thermal as well as acoustic insulation. Additionally it can be used to warm or cool a floatation tank or void space by passing hot or cold water through the hose.

Vibrations

BUILDING VIBRATIONS OWING TO HIGHWAY TRAFFIC and other factors are hard to eliminate. In general, it is best to put the tank or void box on a ground floor so that it is free of the low frequency oscillations within a building structure. Other residual sounds include sub-sonic and very low frequency sonic vibration. The low frequency component of the sound of airplane engines, for example, can come through even though you don't hear the higher frequencies. Earthquakes and other sub-sonic vibrations are of such high amplitude that they will come through any insulation.

Readers experimenting with creating a void box might consult the work of Dr. Arthur Janov who developed the "primal scream" box, a safe place where the screamer could retreat to fully and passionate express internal torment, i.e., wailing and screaming, without being heard. While the scream box was designed to keep sounds in, they may also be used for keeping sounds out.

Heat Flow and Temperature

TEMPERATURE GRADIENTS ACROSS THE FACE, the head, and the rest of the body are very powerful programmers of our states of being. All you have to do is to take off your clothes and move around in the nude for a bit to experience a sudden change in the programming.

In ordinary, everyday life our skin—our periphery—is stimulated by differences in temperature from the feet to the top of the head. The amount of temperature difference at the skin is determined by amount and kind of clothing, humidity, and the temperature of the medium—air, water, snow, or other—in which the body is immersed.

Your subjective appreciation of temperature over the surface of your body varies, within certain physiological limits, by your bio-computer programming. There are various sources of heat inside the body. There are, for example, one hundred billion cells, each one of which produces a little bit of heat while it is living. All of these one hundred billion cells add up to a total body basal metabolism of about eighty watts, in a resting state.

Your subjective appreciation of either cold or heat is the temperature gradient between the inside of your body and your surrounds. In short, your skin temperature has a determining impact on your subjective appreciation of heat or cold. The air humidity determines the amount of cooling by evaporation of perspiration from the skin, which makes it is a powerful determinant of skin temperature.

Body basal metabolism of about eighty watts, in a resting state.

Such heat sources must be eliminated to reduce skin temperature. Here again the flotation tank offers the easiest solution of partial immersion in water of the desired temperature. A coiled garden hold under the tank—or void box—offers a simple ways of regulating temperature.

Humidity

THE AIR ABOVE THE WATER IN THE ISOLATION TANK should be kept near 100 percent humidity, at full saturation to eliminate sensations from perspiration evaporation. Saturating the air with water vapor keeps humidity high and prevents evaporative cooling of the body surfaces the surface of the water. Humidity can be increased in dry void rooms and void boxes with a simple humidifier of the type used to help breathing such as when you have a bad cold or asthma, which is inexpensive and available is most drugstores.

When using a humidifier, make sure to clean it regularly with a disinfectant, like bleach, to prevent the growth of mold, which can be unhealthy to breath. In fact, mold can take root in the flotation tank's airspace as well as in the room or void box. It would be well advised to mist the void space with diluted bleach or hydrogen peroxide before entering. But make sure to wait sufficiently long—5 minutes or so— for the disinfectant mist to dissipate so that you don't breathe it, which would certainly aversely hyperstimulate your lungs, just the opposite of the objective of entering the void space!

Gravity

IN ORDINARY, EVERYDAY ACTIVITY, below our levels of awareness, we are constantly computing the direction of gravity. These computations are carried out within our bio-computer, mainly through the cerebella mechanisms and the inner ear. Under gravitation we are also presuming that computations having to do with inertia, rotational accelerations are included.

In everyday life, the body exerts counter-forces against that of gravity through the muscular-skeletal system. Correct here and now body position is automatically computed through cerebella and other mechanisms. For example, these computations place the feet in just the right position to keep the center of gravity supported at a given height when walking or running. We don't have to pay much attention to these mechanisms; they are automatic.

As we walk, stand, or run, we can see that there is a very small area of contact between our feet and the earth. All of the effect of gravitational pressure is now exerted in this area of the foot; this is maximal anti-gravitational stimulation in the periphery. If you increase the area of contact for the anti-gravity forces, such as by lying down flat on a comfortable bed, you reduce the amount of stimulation or local pressure by gravity on the periphery of the body. You do not reduce it in regard to the inner ear, however. The only way stimulation can be reduced on the inner ear is to move out into a field free of gravity in far-out spaces beyond the solar system, or to go into orbit around the planet, so that the centrifugal force balances the gravitational force. Then the inner ear is free of gravity.

Miscellaneous Stimulation

THE ELECTROMAGNETIC SPECTRUM and its ability to stimulate has not been investigated thoroughly, except for the visible, light region. In the vicinity of powerful radio stations some people's teeth fillings, for example, can rectify the electromagnetic energy and convert it into sonic energy so that they can hear broadcasts through the fillings in their teeth. It is wise to avoid this effect by not putting a tank of void box in the vicinity of a powerful transmitter.

Radio waves of long wavelengths of sufficient intensity can raise body temperature. This process is called *diathermy*. You should not place the tank or use a void space anywhere near a radio source, either of a diathermy or a radar type. Some people can pick up the extremely powerful-beamed radiation from radar transmitters. It is wise not to have the tank or void space in such a field. You can detect whether or not there is such a field present by hooking up a hi-fi amplifier and having an open input with a small antenna. Every time the radar beam sweeps though the area, you will hear the pulsing of the beam through the hi-fi set.

> Certain radio waves of sufficient intensity can raise body temperature.

Sufficient Time

SUFFICIENT TIME and a sufficient number of exposures to sensory solitude—the void— is needed to develop tolerance to one's inner mind. For example, Richard P. Feynman, 1965 Nobel Prize laureate for his research in quantum electrodynamics, exposed himself to thirty-three hours of total tank work over a period of twelve weeks. Only after five hours of work was he able to do the things he wanted, such as moving his conscious center out of his body while in the tank.

Avoid Expectations

THERE IS ALSO A PRE-PROGRAMMING of "expectation effect." If you set a definite time for leaving the tank or desert or cave, or you make an arrangement with another person who is expected to come and interrupt expo-

sure to the void situation, you tend to be programmed
into expecting that person to make that interruption.
For the expectant interval of time, this will determine
to some extent the phenomena that you experience
under these conditions.

Some people arrived at my house expecting us to
give them some form of preprogramming. Others
arrived with their own expectations of what was going
to happen in the void. An amusing anecdote occurred
when a particularly busy and highly energetic man
arrived, didn't have much time to spend, and wanted
to spend it all in my isolation tank. So he hurried
through his shower and climbed into the tank, spent
an hour, came out and hurried through his second
━━━━━━━━━ shower to clean off the Epsom salts
But nothing residue. As he was going out the
happened? door, I said, "Do you have anything
to report about what happened in the
tank?" Very quickly, as he was exiting, he said, "Nothing happened."

I saw many cases like this. In general it seems that
these people arrive with certain expectations. They are
going to accomplish certain things in isolation; there
are going to be far-out trips; they are going to halluci-
nate; they are going to have new and unique experiences.

Some arrived already preprogrammed by what I
wrote about my own experiences in isolation, recounted in *The Center of the Cyclone* and in *Programming
and Metaprogramming in the Human Biocomputer.* When
they say "nothing happened" it means that their
experience did not live up to their own expectations of
what could happen.

Therefore it is recommended that you go into
solitude with a freely floating program, a freely floating schedule, and avoid over-scheduling, either in
terms of immersion or emersion into and from the
void situation.

14
ALTERNITY

THIS IS AN OPERATIONAL STATEMENT and a point of view from a lifetime of work in the tank with and without chemical aids. It is a statement that lays the responsibility for what happens directly on you, the person in the void. In the void space you cannot escape this responsibility by projecting onto others.

> *"In the province of the mind, what one believes to be true, either is true or becomes true within certain limits. These limits are to be found experientially and experimentally. When the limits are determined, it is found that they are further beliefs to be transcended. In the province of the mind, there are no limits."*

—John Lilly

You may try your usual evasions of penetration of Self, you may carry out multiple tape loop dances of all sorts, but you cannot escape the fact that you are alone.

Discovering Metabeliefs

YOUR METABELIEF OPERATOR IS CLEAREST IN A VOID or isolation environment. You have no duties in the external reality whatsoever. You are freed up temporarily from the necessities of schedules, from the programming of others by Self and of Self by others, from the necessities of maintaining the balance of the body under gravitational field, from patterned visual inputs and patterned acoustic inputs. It is only in this environment that the truth of the above metabelief operator can be realized.

I discovered that the sensory void experience is the portal to "hyper-space." I was able to enter it by flotation tank. From there I could jump from one universe to another—from this reality to an alternate reality—while maintaining human structure, size, concepts, and memories. My center of consciousness was here, and yet I could know immediately what was going on anywhere in the universe. In *alternity* all choices are possible.

From my experiences I am convinced that Eastern yoga philosophy is right. There is a purusha or atman—a soul—for each person, for the planet, one for the galaxy, and so on. As mathematician philosopher Franklin Merrill-Wolff says in his book, *The Philosophy of Consciousness Without an Object*, consciousness was first—even before the void. Creation began when consciousness got bored and turned in upon itself, becoming conscious of itself. He-she-it created time, space, energy, matter, male, female—the whole tableau.

> *"They believe that I am what they see me as rather than what they do not see. I am the great unseen. In a sense, I am what I am not. It is from the am-not-ness that I come and to it I always return. "*
>
> —Neal Donald Walsch
> *Conversations with God*

In a few experiments, I personally went through alternate realities and realized that they are a set which are determined from hyperspace by intelligences far greater than ours. By discussing this with these intelligences and moving above hyperspace to the next level with the cooperation of these super intelligences, once I achieved this state of this alternate reality, the Ultimate Alternate Reality, I become part of the mind of God and can look out through the eyes of God at His creation—the whole universe.

I could focus that consciousness down to any extent that I wanted to into a given person, a given animal, a given solar system, a given star, or a given galaxy. I realized that I could know anything, everywhere, all the time and an immense sense of boredom takes place. I realized that all of this is taking place and you are given consciousness in order to explore for my particular purpose "everything that I do must be designed to avoid boring God Himself." So the ultimate alternative reality is avoiding boredom in the mind of God.

If you experience these spaces, you must forget about them when you come back. You must forget you're omnipotent and omniscient and take the game seriously so you'll engage in sex, have children, and participate in the whole human scenario. There's always an extraterrestrial feeling when you come back from a deep sensory void session—or a coma or psychosis, for that matter. You must read the manual in the bio-computer's glove compartment so you can run the human vehicle once more.

Science & God

IN THE FACE OF THE VASTNESS OF THE UNKNOWN, some of us have awe and reverence. In most discussions in science, this factor is neglected. We discuss curiosity, intellect, intuition, genius, truth, power, support, facilities, and facts. Most scientists neglect the inner wellsprings of our own beings in their chosen profession. Professors, assistant professors, and teaching instructors do not have time for this kind of a discussion And yet, practically every student that I knew well said he was there because of these two factors—reverence and awe.

The sensitive humanist in me says there are vast areas of ignorance and of ignorings in this part of me, this scientist part. This humanist side says there is more than our science has yet dared to dream of. Our current knowledge is a very thin closed shell surrounding our minds with vast unknowns inside it and outside it.

If some other species with a different logic and mathematics tried hard to teach us, probably we couldn't recognize and learn the alien ways of thought and computation. We tend to ignore the possibilities of thought outside the traditional prescriptions for thinking.

My sorrow for the young human is great. Why cannot their genius flower as it will? We straitjacket the young and penalize the thinking they do outside our beaten and beat up paths inherited from the past.

We should be concerned with the forces in the young people going into science. We should be concerned with their ethics, their morals, and their motivations. The whole future of our civilization is in their hands. Unless we aid the youngsters to see the necessity of awe, reverence, and respect, they can become dangerously calloused and cynical, not only in their scientific work, but in the application of their scientific work to technology. With more reverence for all of life, with more awe in the face of the inside unknown and the outside unknown, with deeper experiences with other human beings from the far side of the planet, maybe the bombs would never have been needed and hence not made or planned.

Most scientists neglect the inner wellsprings of our own beings.

State of High Indifference

IN THE VOID I SAW THE POSSIBILITY of experiencing my planet side trip in a state of High Indifference, of *Nirvana, Samadhi,* or *Satori.* Perhaps if a sufficiently large number embrace this set of meta-programs we may survive our alternative dichotomous love of righteous wrath. It may be that High Indifference is a reasonable alternative to righteous wrath which is a non-surviving program for the human species.

Setting up a hierarchy of states of consciousness with High Indifference at the top, *Nirvana* next, *Satori* next, *Samadhi* next, and *Ananda* at the bottom is an interesting game, especially when one becomes capable of moving through all these spaces and staying in each sufficiently long enough to know it.

This may be a better game than killing our neighbors because they do not believe in our simulations of God. At least those who espouse these states claim that these states are above any other human aspiration; that once we have experienced them, we are almost unfit for wrath, for pride, for arrogance, for power over others, for group pressure exerted either upon ourselves or upon others. We become fit only for teaching these states to those who are ready to learn them.

The *bodhisattva* vow is no longer necessary for those who have had direct experience. We become the *bodhisattva* without the vow. We becomes Buddha without being Buddha.

We become content with the minimum necessities for survival on the planet-side trip. We cut back on the use of unnecessary articles—machines, gadgets, and devices. We no longer need motion pictures, television, dishwashers, or other luxuries. We no longer need much of what most people value above all else. We no longer need the excitement of war. We no longer need to be a slave to destructive thoughts or deeds. We no longer need to organize.

God as Consciousness-Without-an-Object, if real, will be apperceived and introcepted by more and more as we turn toward the inner realities within each of us. If God as Consciousness-Without-an-Object inhabits each of us, we eventually will see this. We will become universally aware. We will realize consciousness as being everywhere and eternal. We will realize that Consciousness-Without-an-Object in each of us is prejudiced and biased because it has linked up with a human brain.

Freeing Up the Spirit

I LEARNED TO VALUE THE FREEING UP OF THE SPIRIT. In this freeing, I was penalized by my own straitjacket. Tradition and personal history are terrible taskmasters with entirely too much power over one's sprit. I sought means of loosening the slave's chains with the hope that eventually I could see the new vistas through the prison window.

Each man has a mind beyond reach of present scientific knowledge. This mind is larger than the man himself conceives of or/and is larger than he is conceived by his fellow man. Our minds have depths beyond our present ken. Parts of the mind reach beyond our own conscious comprehension and beyond the prescribed consciousness of our time. With special techniques and special knowledge we can travel through the vastnesses of our minds locked within our brains. Much romantic nonsense is stored in our minds. Courage is needed to get rid of this romantic nonsense.

> Each man has a mind beyond reach of present scientific knowledge.

Once we have been through deep experiences in tune with the vast forces of the universe, the vast forces within ourselves, we see that the need for conflict, the need for hostility, and the need for hatred become less intense. We find the universe inside and the outside so vast and so lonely that any other living thing that loves or shows any signs of loving is precious and close. Our own inner discontents show up as the trivial conflicts that they really are. Time on this earth is of immense value beyond the small grievances, the bickerings, the complaints, the encroachments, and the fools. Time here is for exploration of the unknowns. If, at the time of the death of each of our bodies, the spirit also dies, then this time is incredibly precious.

> "The mercy of the West has been social revolution; the mercy of the East has been individual insight into the basic self/void. We need both. They are both contained in the traditional three aspects of the Dharma path: wisdom (prajna), meditation (dhyana), and morality (sila). Wisdom is intuitive knowledge of the mind of love and clarity that lies beneath one's ego-driven anxieties and aggressions. Meditation is going into the mind to see this for yourself—over and over again, until it becomes the mind you live in. Morality is bringing it back out in the way you live, through personal example and responsible action, ultimately toward the true community (sangha) of "all beings."
>
> —Gary Snyder
> *Buddhist Anarchism*

It's all the time we have for each one of us. If the spirit lives on here or elsewhere and continues to send and receive information, this time may also be precious and incredibly important. Our behavior, our achievements, the marks that we make now may or may not determine what sort of an after life we may have. I don't know which of these alternatives is the real truth. I do know that it is important to spend our time now on important projects.

15

SENSORY DEPRIVATION

I SOUGHT ANSWERS TO THE QUESTION of what happens to a brain and its contained-mind in the relative absence of physical stimulation—the sensory void. In neurophysiology, this is one form of the question: Freed of normal efferent and afferent activities, does the activity of the brain soon become that of coma or sleep? Or is there an inherent mechanism which keeps it going, a pacemaker of the "awake" type of activity? In psychoanalysis, there is a similar, but not identical, question. If the healthy ego is freed of reality stimuli, does it maintain the secondary process, or does primary process take over? Is the healthy ego independent of reality or dependent in some fashion, in some degree, on exchanges with the surroundings to maintain its structure?

In seeking answers, I found pertinent autobiographical literature and reports of experiments by others, and conducted experiments myself. The experiments were psychological ones on human subjects. Many psychological experiments have been done on animals kept in isolation. The effect on very young animals can be an almost completely irreversible lack of development of physical whole systems, such as those necessary for the use of vision in accomplishing tasks.

In the 1950s, several research projects were started that were called "sensory deprivation." In my experience in the tank which provided physical isolation, there was no psychological state that can be termed "sensory deprivation." In the absence of sensory input and physical output, I found no "deprived" states except those created by self meta-programming. The latter are re-programmable into richly elaborate states of inner experience.

> In the absence of sensory input and physical output, I found no "deprived" states except those created by self meta-programming.

The term "sensory deprivation" was invented by psychologists who did not do self-investigation and who did experiments on subjects, expecting a "deprivation state" in the isolated circumstances. In my void state research with over three hundred subjects I found no such states of "deprivation," nor the predicated "stress" of physical isolation.

I examined the literature on the effects of extended periods, from weeks to months, of solitude in small boats on oceans, in the polar night, and came to the conclusion that physical dangers combined with solitude are very stressful. This does not say that physical isolation and solitude without danger are stressful. This confusion between factors responsible has been perpetuated in the sensory deprivation literature.

My research showed that when you eliminate external sources of low-level pain and sources of danger, the inner experience—the inperience—can be anything that you can allow yourself to experience. My subjects reported mostly "self-programmed" or "spontaneous" experiences rather than fear-filled, stressful, deprived ones. The complete comfort of the isothermal supportive bath in the dark and the silence affords a complete physical-mental-spiritual resting place, which can contain a great peace for those ready for it.

Isolation Research

THE LONGEST EXPOSURE TO ISOLATION on the largest number of subjects was carried out by Dr. Donald Hebb at
McGill University. Subjects were placed on a bed in an
air-conditioned box with arms and hands restrained
with cardboard sleeves, and eyes covered completely
with translucent ski goggles. The aim was to reduce
the patterning of stimuli to the lowest level. The
subjects were college students motivated by receiving
monitary payment as long as they stayed in the box.

> **An extreme desire for stimuli and action developed.**

An observer was present, watching
through a window, and tested the
subject in various ways verbally
through a communication set.

Hebb's subjects varied considerably in the details of their experiences.
However, a few general phenomena
appeared. After several hours, his subjects found that
it was difficult to carry on organized, directed thinking
for any sustained period. Suggestibility was very
much increased. An extreme desire for stimuli and
action developed. There were periods of thrashing
around in the box in attempts to satisfy this need. The
borderline between sleep and wakefulness became
diffuse and confused. At some time between 24 and 72
hours most subjects couldn't stand it any longer and
left. Hallucinations and delusions of various sorts
developed, mostly in those who could stay longer than
two days.

Hallucinations

THE DEVELOPMENT OF HALLUCINATIONS that the subjects
experienced in the visual sphere followed the stages
seen in mescaline intoxication. When full-blown, the
visual phenomena were complete, three-dimensional
projections. The hallucination contents consisted of
material like that of dreams, connected stories sharing

past memories, and recent real events. The subjects'
reactions to these phenomena were generally amuse-
ment and a sense of relief from the pressing boredom.
They could describe them vocally without abolishing
the sequences. A small number of subjects experienced doubling of their body images. A few developed transient paranoid delusions, and one had a
seizure-like episode after five days in the box with no
positive EEG findings for epilepsy.

Lilly Research

IN MY EXPERIMENTS, SUBJECTS WERE IMMERSED in a tank
containing slowly flowing water at 34.2 C (93.5 F).
They wore a blacked-out mask that enclosed the whole
head for breathing and no clothes. My objective was to
reduce the absolute intensity of all physical stimuli to
the lowest possible level. The water temperature was
such that the subjects felt neither hot nor cold. A large
fraction of the usual pressures on the body caused by
gravity are lacking so that tactually, subjects felt the
supports and the mask, but not much else.

The sound level was low because water-air interface does not transmit air-borne sounds very effi-
ciently. Subjects could hear only their own breathing
and some faint water sounds from the piping. It was
an even and monotonous environments. After the
initial training period, no observer was present. Immediately after exposure in "the tank," subjects wrote
personal notes on their experience.

My experiments were more limited both in numbers of subjects and duration of exposures. There were
two subjects with the longest exposure being three
hours. Subjects always had a full night's rest before
entering the tank. Before entering the tank they were
instructed to inhibit all movements as far as possible.
An initial set of training exposures helped overcome
the fears of the situation itself.

For about the first three-quarters of an hour, the day's residues are predominant. The subjects reported being aware of the surroundings, recent problems, and so on. Gradually, they begin to relax and more or less enjoy the experience. The feeling of being isolated in space and having nothing to do is restful and relaxing at this stage. Slowly, during the next hour, a tension develops which can be called a "stimulus-action" hunger; hidden methods of self-stimulation develop, such as twitching muscles, slow swimming movements, which cause sensations as the water flows by the skin, stroking one finger with another, and so forth. Sometimes the tension developed to the point of forcing the subject to leave the tank. We found that if such maneuvers were inhibited long enough, intense satisfaction was derived from later self-simulations.

Meanwhile, the attention was drawn powerfully to any residual stimulus. The mask, the suspension, each come in for their share of concentration. Such residual stimuli become the whole content of consciousness to an almost unbearable degree. If this stage was passed without leaving the tank, subjects noticed that their thoughts shifted from a directed type of thinking about problems to reveries and fantasies of a highly personal and emotionally charged nature.

Exposure to tank experiences trains us to be more tolerant of many internal activities.

When the tension and the fantasies are withstood, subjects may experience the furthest stage—projection of visual imagery. The black curtain in front of the eyes, such as one "sees" in a dark room with eyes closed, gradually opened out into a three-dimensional, dark, empty space in front of the body. Gradually forms sometimes seen in hypnogogic states appeared.

It turns out that exposure to such conditions trains us to be more tolerant of many internal activities. Fear lessens with experience, and personal integration can be speeded up. Breathing in the tank was extremely important as a comforting, constant safeguard and a source of rhythmic stimulation.

After Effects

IN BOTH THE MCGILL EXPERIMENTS AND IN MINE, certain after effects were noted. The McGill subjects had difficulty in orienting their perceptual mechanisms and various illusions persisted for several hours. In my experiments, I noticed that after emersion, the day apparently started over. The subjects reported feeling as if they had just arisen from bed afresh. This effect persisted as subjects found themselves out of step with the clock for the rest of that day. Social intercourse had to be readjusted in subtle ways. The night of the day of the exposure subjects said that their beds exerted great pressure against their body, for example. No bed is a comfortable as floating in water.

16

POLAR & SEA-FARING ISOLATION

COLLECTED EIGHTEEN AUTOBIOGRAPHICAL CASES from the polar and sea-faring literature which are more frank and revealing than most. From this literature I found that isolation per se acts on most persons as a powerful stress. The effects observed are similar to those of any extreme stress. Other stressful factors add their effects to those of isolation to cause mental symptoms to appear more rapidly and more intensely. As is well known, stresses other than isolation can cause the same symptoms to appear in individuals in an isolated group.

Taking our last point first, we have the account by Walter Gibson given in his book, *The Boat*, in which four persons out of an initial 135 survived in a lifeboat in the Indian Ocean in World War II. Gibson gives a vivid account of his experiences, and the symptoms resulting from loss of hope, dehydration, thirst, intense sunburn, and physical combat. Most of the group hallucinated rescue planes and drank salt water thinking it fresh; many despaired and committed suicide; others were murdered; and some were eaten by others. The whole structure of egos was shaken and recast in desperate efforts at survival. It is interesting to note that many of those who committed suicide tried to sink the boat by removing the drain plugs before jumping overboard.

I cite this case because it gives a clue as to what to expect in those who do survive isolation in other conditions. Gibson said he survived because he had previously had training in withstanding tropical sun for some years. Additionally, Gibson tells how he had previously learned to be able to become completely passive physically and mentally. Another factor critical to his survival was having the conviction that he would come through the experience; and, I add, by having a woman, Doris Lim, beside him, who shared his passivity and convictions.

In all cases of isolation survivors, at sea or in the polar night, the first exposure caused the greatest fears and hence the greatest danger of giving way to symptoms. Previous experience was a powerful aid in going ahead, despite the symptoms. Physical passivity was necessary during starvation. However passivity may be contra-indicated in social isolation in the absence of starvation. All survivors held an inner conviction that they would survive, or there were definite reassurances from others that each would be rescued.

> If the terror of the first week can be overcome, one can survive.

In cases of a man and a woman together, there was not only a real assurance of survival, but a love of the situation appeared. Such love can develop in a solitaire. Of course, such coupling is psychologically the antithesis complete isolation—an experience devoid of all sensory input/output including communication with others. Many symptoms are avoided by healthy persons with such a coupling arrangement.

Alone at Sea

SOLITARY SAILORS ARE IN A MORE COMPLEX SITUATION than the group of polar isolates. The sailing of a small boat across oceans requires a good deal of physical exertion, and the situation may be contaminated by a lack of sleep, which can also cause symptoms. The solitary sailors, of which Joshua Slocum and Alain Bombard are outstanding examples, relate that the first days out of port are the dangerous ones. Awe, humility, and fear in the face of the sea are most acute at this time. Bombard states that if the terror of the first week can be overcome, one can survive.

Apparently, many do not survive this first period. Many single-handed boats have not arrived at their transoceanic destination. We have clues as to the causes from what sometimes happens with two persons on such crossings. There are several accounts of pairs of ocean-crossing sailors in which one of the couple became so terror-stricken, paranoid, and bent on murder and/or suicide, that he had to be tied to his bunk.

When this first period is past, other symptoms develop, from isolation itself or from isolation exacerbated by other stresses. In the South Atlantic, Joshua Slocum had a severe gastro-intestinal upset just before a gale hit his boat. He had reefed his sails, but should have taken them down. He was physically unable to move from the cabin when he saw a man take over the tiller. At first he thought it was a pirate, but the man reassured him and said that he was the pilot of the Pinta and that he would take his boat safely through the storm. Slocum asked him to take down sail, but the man said, no, they must catch the Pinta ahead.

The next morning Slocum recovered, and found his boat had covered 93 miles on true course, sailing itself. His boat was quite capable of such a performance because he arranged it that way for long trips without his hand at the helm. In a dream that night the pilot appeared and said he would come whenever Slocum needed him. During the next three years the helmsman appeared to Slocum several times during gales.

This type of hallucination-delusion seems to be characteristic of the strong egos who survive. They exhibit a "savior" type of hallucination rather than a "destroyer" type. Their inner conviction of survival is projected thoroughly.

Superstitiousness often appears. Slocum thought a dangerous reef named M Reef was lucky because M is the 13th letter of the alphabet and 13 was his lucky number. He passed the reef without hitting it.

Superstitiousness often appears.

Bombard thought the number of matches necessary to light a damp cigarette represented the number of days until the end of the voyage. He was wrong several times.

Characteristics of Survivors

ISOLATION SURVIVORS DESCRIBE AN INTENSE LOVE of all living things. Slocum was revolted at the thought of killing food-animals, especially a goat given to him at one port. Ellam and Mudie became quite upset after catching and eating a fish that had followed the boat all day, and swore off further fish-eating.

Isolation survivors tell of having conversations with inanimate objects. Bombard had bilateral conversations with a doll mascot.

Time to Adjust

DURING ISOLATION INNER LIFE BECOMES SO VIVID and intense that it takes time to readjust to the life among other people and to reestablish one's inner criteria of sanity. When placed with fellow prisoners, after 18 months in solitary confinement, Christopher Burney was afraid to speak for fear that he would show himself to be insane. After several days of listening he recaptured the usual criteria of sanity, finally allowing himself to speak.

Survivors describe feeling that when they land, they must be careful to listen before speaking to avoid being considered insane. Bernicot refused an invitation to dinner on another yacht after crossing the Atlantic alone, until he could recapture the proper things to talk about.

Life alone in the polar night, snowed-in, with the confining surroundings of a small hut is a more simple situation than the sailor out at sea alone in a small boat. However, there are still complicating factors, including extreme cold, possibilities of carbon monoxide poisoning, collapse of the roof under the weight of the snow, and so forth. Richard Byrd, in his book, *Alone*, recounts in great detail his changes in mental functioning, and talks of a long period of carbon monoxide poisoning resulting in a state close to catatonia. Like Slocum and many others, he experienced an oceanic feeling—the being at one with the universe.

Christiane Ritter, who wrote *A Woman in the Polar Night*, was exposed to isolation for periods up to 16 days at a time. She saw a monster, hallucinated her past as if in bright sunshine, became "at one" with the moon, and developed a monomania to go out over the snow. She was saved by an experienced Norwegian who put her to bed and fed her lavishly. She developed a love for the situation and found great difficulty in leaving Spitzbergen.

Like Mental Illness

PUBLISHED AUTOBIOGRAPHIES are of necessity incomplete. Social taboos, discretion to one's self, suppression and repression of painful or uncomfortable material, secondary elaboration, and rationalization severely limit the scope of the material available. Despite these limitations, we find that people in isolation experiences exhibit many symptoms of the mentally ill. In those who survive, the symptoms can be reversible. How easily reversible, we do not know. Most survivors report, after several weeks exposure to isolation, a new inner security and a new integration of themselves on a deep and basic level.

> In those who survive, the symptoms can be reversible.

The underlying mechanisms are obscure. It is obvious that inner factors in the mind tend to be projected outward, that some of the mind's activity, which is usually reality-bound, becomes free to turn to fantasy, including hallucination and delusion. It is as if the laws of thought are projected into the realm of the laws of inanimate matter and of the universe. Such experiences lead to improved mental functioning or to destruction. Why one person takes the healthy path and another person the sick one is not clear.

17

EVOLUTION

THE MIND CONTAINED WITHIN THE BRAIN is the result of the evolutionary process occurring on this planet. The proper atoms accumulated in this portion of the universe at the proper distance from the sun, at the proper temperature. The coalescence of the atoms into a planet, into an atmosphere, into water upon the surface of that planet formed the seas and oceans. The storms over the ocean produced lightning, streaking through the atmosphere and forming nitrogen compounds which fell into the ocean; there combining with the carbon of carbon dioxide, the atoms coalesced into long chains of peptides and eventually proteins. The peptides and the proteins formed small balls of peculiar construction. These balls floated in the bosom of the primordial soup of the seas. The balls coalesced, joined one another, incorporated a new structure. The new structure became the primordial viruses; the viruses joined, became the first bacteria. The bacteria accumulated further layers and became the first protozoan cells. The protozoans joined in colonies, forming the first sponges and the first coral. Evolution proceeded over millions of years, resulting in the worms, the starfish, the tunicates.

Within these organisms new cells developed, specialized for conduction of nervous impulses. The prototype of the nervous system began to evolve in the jellyfish, the worms, the starfish, the tunicates. The fish evolved, the nervous system moved toward the head end of the new organisms. The distance receptors, the eyes, the lateral-line organs all became oriented forward in the direction of motion. The lungfish evolved, climbed out on the land, and looked at the new territory. The amphibians evolved in the sea, climbed out on the land, became adapted to a combined dry-land water existence. The reptiles evolved from the amphibians. Some reptiles returned to the sea and slowly but surely evolved into huge forms which gradually became the primitive dolphins and whales. The nervous system grew and, in the whales, evolved to the size of the humans to come fifty million years later.

The reptiles on the land gave rise to the first landborne mammals. The mammals climbed in the trees and grew. Their brains grew larger as they evolved into the monkeys, the apes, the human species in the prototypic form. The prototype humans evolved further, increasing their brain mass. Meanwhile, in the sea, the dolphins and whales evolved larger nervous systems that equaled the present human one thirty million years ago.

Large Brains

IN EACH OF THE LARGE EVOLVED ANIMALS, including the human, were brains now capable of new choices, of new directions, of new control over the environment and over the Self. The contained mind, as we know it today, evolved to its present complex distribution.

> As Man became aware of his own awareness he developed delusions of grandeur.

As Man became aware of his own awareness, as Man became aware of his own brain, as Man became aware that he was interdependent with other men, as Man built, created, and lived in his human consensus reality, he lost contact with his planet. He developed delusions of grandeur in which he was the preeminent species. He gave himself a special creation and a special evolution separate from that of the planet and from the other creatures created upon it by the evolutionary process.

Man created a special origin for himself. He represented his consciousness as a "soul." The soul was a divine portion of God, the God that he had created in his own contained mind. Man assumed that his mind was part of a Universal Mind, uncontained in any brain. Man peopled his external reality with simulations of the operations of minds greater than his. Man worshiped these minds. He organized churches. He wrote books. He wrote handbooks of God, called the *Bible*, the *Koran*, the *Sutras*, the *Vedas*, the *Upanishads*.

> Man created a special origin for himself and represented his consciousness as a "soul."

Various men and women went into solitude, into hermitages, into remote cells, into caves, into the deserts and experienced realities which they called spiritual. Their minds contained in their brains generated experiences beyond the planet, beyond their human form, beyond their understanding.

Man Explored Man

SLOWLY MAN BEGAN TO INVESTIGATE his own material nature. He studied his brain. He studied damaged human brains. He studied the results of damage to brains. He explored the inner realities of those with intact brains, those with small brains, those with large brains. He traced his own genetic code, his inheritance carried forward in his three-billion-year evolution from primordial matter. He studied the complex assemblages of that matter. He investigated the primitive particles giving rise to that matter. He studied the molecular configurations present in living organisms and in his own body and brain.

Man's evolution began to be what Man conceived it to be: what he thought his fellowman was, his human organizations were, his speech, writing, computers, and the vast diversity of beliefs about self were. Man warred on Man. Man killed Man. Man killed other organisms on the planet by the hundreds of thousands and the millions. Man's own thoughts of himself were as a divinely special creature, evolved and designed to exploit the planet for his own survival and economic gain. His laws were designed to regulate his behavior with regard to other humans and to control the other organisms as if they were a part of his own divinely inherited property. He domesticated many animals; those who could not be domesticated were killed.

The extinction of species proceeded rapidly. Finally some men became aware that if this course continued, the planet would be bereft of many species, many more than those that had already become extinct through Man's efforts. The whales and dolphins of the sea were being killed in the name of the economic religion of Man. His conceit that other species were an economic resource for his exploitation was killing off huge cultures, huge histories of which Man was not yet aware. Man's development of speech and man-to-man communication isolated him from the possibilities of communication with other brains as large as his and larger than his. The whale and dolphin cultures were being decimated, their histories stored in their huge brains decimated, as the oldest and largest of the whales were selected for slaughter.

> I felt as if I were in a human trap.

Trapped

As I REVIEWED THIS HISTORY I felt as if I were in a human trap, constructed over the millennia. I thought, "I am merely one of billions of humans. How can I possibly influence the evolution of this planet? Belief is fighting belief in the human reality. Is what I believe to be true, true, any more than what others believe to be true? Is my ignorance any smaller than the ignorance of others? My knowledge feels so small! I want to enlarge it. I am enlarging it, and a temporary set of beliefs to enlarge my knowledge is necessary. Those beliefs can be changed as the knowledge accumulates.

What are the paths to knowledge? We as humans need to communicate with others than ourselves to escape this trap of the closed system of our own communication: this trap of our own competitions, of our human-to-human warfare, of our human-to-human dogmatic beliefs, of our human-to-human lethality, of our human-to-other-species lethality. We must control our killing, our devastation, and develop understanding. How can I best effect this?

> My knowledge feels so small! I want to enlarge it.

For the acquisition of new knowledge one needs the cooperation of selected humans, self-selected humans. Humans with discipline, humans with knowledge of science, humans with flexible new belief systems beyond those which have kept us in our present prison of belief. Knowledge of brain. The alternatives open to large brains, especially those beyond our own. If the mind is contained in the brain, then the size of that mind is a definite function of the size of that brain. The number of alternatives open to a mind is a function of how large the brain is in which it is contained.

The uncontained mind belief, if true, then says that what the mind has available to it through the vehicle in which it resides is a function of the size of the brain available to that mind. The material valve for Universal Mind regulates the amount of revelation, the amount of knowledge which can be squeezed through that valve.

19

MAKING SENSE
OF IT ALL

SWING FROM CONTAINED TO UNCONTAINED MIND and back to contained mind. I swing from belief in the three Beings to the simulation of these Beings as a convenient method of thought to free up my thinking. Belief versus experience. Is belief any truer than experience? Is direct inner experience truer than direct outer experience? Are the consensus beliefs applied to belief itself and to experience itself, inner and outer, valid?

I feel that I am merely an agent giving you some keys which have been given to me to pass on to you. These keys are to unlock doors out of you present prison. Doors opening on new vistas. Doors beyond where you are now.

In general, the theme of these writings is that each one of us is far greater, far more advanced, far more consciously aware, far more intelligent, than each one of us conceives of our selves as being.

Who are the whales, dolphins, and porpoises? Will we ever know? We won't know until we break the communication barrier with them. I hope we are capable of doing that before it is too late, before there are no Cetacea left to communicate with.

Third Being: *"Looking at the details of the conscious programming of the agent on Earth, I suggest that we arrange for certain kinds of coincidences for him as demonstrations of our control.*

I also suggest that we use another agent on the planet Earth to control short-term coincidences in a particular direction for my agent. The second agent that I suggest using is a young medical doctor who is the best friend of my agent. This young medical doctor has been doing experiments along the lines of those my agent was doing much earlier in the tank with chemical agents. He is twenty years younger than my agent. He has become acquainted with various means of changing his own belief systems flexibly and open-endedly. He has means at his disposal to open up my human agent's mind to new possibilities."

Second Being: *"I have been in communication with the Being in control of this friend of your agent. The control Being for the young medical doctor will cooperate in this as a joint venture in terms of our agents on Earth."*

First Being: *"It is apparent then that the agent about whom we are conferring is ready for a new series of teachings. We must arrange these coincidences in such a way that he can maintain his life on Earth. Do you feel that he is prepared to go through new experiences for the period of one rotation of the planet Earth about its sun without killing his vehicle?"*

Third Being: *"Obviously he is willing to take rather dangerous chances with his vehicle. If we are to maintain this agent on the planet Earth, we must arrange coincidences to prevent his demise as a human being. We have a number of allies in other agents on Earth who can intervene at the appropriate times. The group of young medical doctors, led by my vehicle and by the other young medical doctor we were speaking of, have held meetings and can be used in our coincidence controls. One or two older ones can serve the function of maintaining the continuity of life in my vehicle."*

First Being: *"Then we are in agreement. This agent is to be put through a new teaching course. We are to arrange the longterm coincidences for survival of his vehicle and prevention of damage to his bio-computer. I hope that you can carry out this."*

If My Mind is Contained

IF MY MIND IS CONTAINED WITHIN MY BRAIN, then the three Beings are either leakages of information into a leaky mind, or they are constructed simulations for unknown purposes, created within my own brain from sources not yet available to me consciously. As Freud would say, they are constructions from my unconscious, generated by belief systems put into me as a child.

If my mind constained in the brain is leaky to sources of information, within our science, then there may be other intelligences in this universe with whom we can communicate and do communicate when we are in the proper state of consciousness and proper state of being. If the mind and the brain are leaky, then

they are available for networks of communication
beyond our present understanding. If the mind is
uncontained, then the Beings have an objective, verifi-
able existence which others can also share. If I believe
in the uncontained mind, then the program I have
outlined here can be believed by some others, and we can have a parallel
programming into my belief system in which the Beings are "real." Thus we
construct another simulated reality as if true.

If our minds
are really
uncontained,
then there is
no science;
there is only
education of
us by the
Universal
Mind.

If the mind in the brain has
sources of information beyond the
present science, then there is something or someone communicating with
us. We arbitrarily assign descriptions
of this someone or something which
correspond to ourselves. We project our simulations on
the information coming in to us from unknown
sources.

If our minds are really uncontained, then there is
no science; there is only education of us by the Universal Mind. Our brains are limited valves, cloaking what
works on this planet with what is fed to us but does
not work on this planet. If we believe that what works
is all there is, then we close our minds and contain
them in order to do the empirical job of surviving and
generate the illusion of a human evolution on this
planet.

Sometimes I believe we are alone in this universe,
that we are strictly an accident, that we originated in
the primordial soup of the seas, and that matter has its
own evolutionary laws which are dimly understood
by us, who are a product of that evolution. Maybe
Earth is the only incubator of life as we know it in the
whole galaxy. If this thought is true, then we merely
construct dreams from the noise of our own brains and

from the cosmic noise of our radio telescopes. If this thought is real, then we are only projecting that which we create within our bio-computers back onto the universe and back onto our own structure.

Freud wrote in his discussion of religion, called *The Future Of an Illusion*, "No, science is no illusion. But it is an illusion to suppose that we can get anywhere else what science cannot give us."

Profound Ignorance

IS THIS MY TRUE BELIEF? If so, my ignorance is profound. Science has not yet been able to construct models of us, models of the universe, which are satisfactory. My hunger for simulations of reality which work is not satisfied. Science to me is open-ended, not closed. The unknown is still with me; my ignorance is still vast. My knowledge is so small, so puny, so weak, can I somehow escape the narcissistic human-centered sources of knowledge and move into new knowledge with other species?

> If I am projecting the Beings, at least I did use this simulation as an inspiration and as a source of opening my mind to new potentialities.

I always seem to end on this question. It is time to do something about it in a way that is demonstrable to others with sufficient knowledge to realize new methods. The new methods that I conceived of must be made real in the form of hardware to solve the problems of inter-species communication. I spent years developing methods.

If I am projecting the Beings, at least I did use this simulation as an inspiration and as a source of opening my mind to new potentialities within the possible and within the probable, making real what is possible to make real in the future, sharing it with those other humans who are also involved in scientific demonstrations.

AUTHOR BIOS

John C. Lilly, M.D., was a pioneering scientist in the fields of consciousness, mind-altering drugs such as LSD and ketamine, and animal intelligence. He was also a noted physician and psychoanalyst and worked extensively in various fields of science, including biophysics, neurophysiology, electronics, and neuroanatomy. Lilly conducted studies on solitude, isolation and confinement and spent twelve years researching dolphin-human relationships. He was associated with the National Institute of Mental Health (NIMH), and the Esalen Institute in California. He taught for—or was affiliated with—CalTech, University of Pennsylvania School of Medicine, was Associate Professor at the University of Pennsylvania, and worked in psychoanalysis at the Institute of the Philadelphia Association for Psychoanalysis and Washington-Baltimore Psychoanalytic Institute and at NIMH. He founded and directed the

Allen Ginsberg, Timothy Leary & John Lilly

Communications Research Institute. In 1954, he invented the Isolation Tank Method.

Lilly's work on dolphin intelligence was the subject of a 1973 film, *The Day of the Dolphin*, starring George C. Scott. His work in developing and experimenting with isolation tanks was the subject of the 1980 film *Altered States* (directed by Ken Russel, starring William Hurt).

Lilly as a young scientist

Devoted to a philosophical quest for the nature of reality, Lilly pursued a brilliant academic career among the scientific leaders of the day. He has lived in the

John Lilly with Ram Dass and Robert Anton Wilson

company of associates and intimates including Nobel physicists Richard Feynman and Robert Milliken, philosophers Buckminster Fuller, Aldous Huxley, and Alan Watts, psychotherapy pioneers R.D. Laing and Fritz Perls, spiritual teachers Oscar Ichazo and Baba Ram Dass, and a host of luminaries, inventors, writers, and Hollywood celebrities.

Philip Bailey

Philip Hansen Bailey Lilly is John Lilly's adopted son. He was trained in Sociology, at UCLA and spent much of the 1980's and 1990's traveling the globe studying current research methods into the theories and practices of human consciousness, dolphin and whale communication and protection, biosystems engineering, poetry, music and the environment. Along the way, his research led to meetings and ongoing projects with Allen Ginsberg, Timothy Leary, Albert Hofmann, and John Allen of the Biosphere II Project.

Philip lived with and assisted John Llly as his personal secretary during the last eleven years of Lilly's life. Philip holds a MBA and manages Lilly's literary rights. He has compiled a CD of recorded music, entitled, *The Dream's Not Over*, on ECCO-Records, available through eccodisc@hotmail.com.

John Lilly with his adopted chldren, Philip Bailey Lilly and Barbara Clark Lilly

Ronin Books
by John Lilly

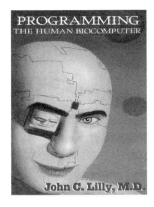

Programming the Human Biocomputer
ISBN 1-57951-065-5
144 pg. $12.95
A new revised editions of Lilly's sought after classic.

The Scientist
A Metaphysical
Autobiography
ISBN 0-914171-72-0
234 pg. $14.95
Lilly's candid story of his life and amazing discoveries.

The Quiet Center
ISBN 1-57951-059-0
144 pg. $12.95
How Lilly discovered a portal to alternative realities—alternity—and what he found there.

HOLY WATER

Cure For The Visionary Blues

The wholeness of all living things
In a Divine Universe
The Mystery of Our Souls
That's the Connection we were seeking
Sanctity in our lives
And freedom from our fears
Beyond the wages of war and ignorance
Searching for the New Jerusalem
Where the Lion lay down with the Lamb
Affirming our destinies
Among green and gentle rolling hills
Outside the bounds of a three dimensional world
Where nothing could hold us back
We breathed enchantment and glory
Beatitude Abounding!
With Visionary Flights through Infinite Space.

In this life there were no guarantees
Which was the right road, if there ever was a right road...
We were never too sure.
Mistakes were a part of the bargain
They made us grow
And we became more powerful
Enduring and prevailing through Noble Truths and Victories
Suffering terrible defeats
Trying not to control fate, but to let it happen
It ain't why, it just Is...

So we slept off the years of our wanderlust
In that shady manor near the River Wye
And loved each other 'til our hearts were filled.
The dearness of the Holy Running Water blessed our souls
And made us whole again
On that bright and blue Palm Sunday
In the ancient village, near the castle walls
The same water that purified our minds in Sunny California
Where birds flew in reoccurring psychedelic patterns.

We thanked the Universe for the journey To The East
And it was right to give it thanks and praise
For the meadows and the churchyard
The dreams that brought us together in communion
To the bridge that helped us make the transition
From this life to the next
On Earth and in the Heavens...
Questing the Everlasting Grail.

—Philip Hansen Balley Lilly

Each one of us is far greater, far more advanced, far more consciously aware, far more intelligent than we conceive of our Selves as being.